Nicky began her Shamanic journey in her early twenties. She appreciates that applying this wisdom to daily life is a continuous path of refining, improving and becoming more consciously aware. She knows the gold medal is waking up to how much power we each have to make a difference in our lives.

For my mum, Gillian, who passed away from this world to continue her journey on 21st April, 2012 – the wisest woman I have ever known.

Nicola Mott

YES, SHAMAN CAN WEAR JEANS

AUSTIN MACAULEY PUBLISHERS™

LONDON • CAMBRIDGE • NEW YORK • SHARJAH

A CIP catalogue record for this title is available from the British Library.

ISBN 9781787104501 (Paperback)
ISBN 9781787104518 (E-Book)

www.austinmacauley.com

First Published (2018)
Austin Macauley Publishers Ltd.
25 Canada Square
Canary Wharf
London
E14 5LQ

Acknowledgments

I only feel I want to mention that really this is for my mum. Four years after her passing away I am still shifting the way in which this book sounds and now seems the time to get it out of my computer and into other people's hands. This goes to those who have cherished and shared so much willingly and open-heartedly.

Also, thank you to everyone at Austin Macauley who have made the publication of this book possible.

I want to emphasize that what I have shared is my experience and interpretation of these ways as they have unfolded and informed me in my own life, and continue to do so. The origins may come from way back in our history but truly the wisdom is as essential to our evolution now as it has always been. I do hope that even if it is in one small way something in this book is of use to you.

For more information you can visit:

www.everydayshaman.uk

Why Don't We Know This?

The very nature of this book owes its creation to the exposure I have experienced to many teachers whose philosophies and generosity have influenced me greatly.

And the feedback I have received when doing workshops has been 'why don't we know this?' So the title of this book is all about us realizing that we all have the potential to take charge of our lives using the tools of the shaman.

There are many great books written by incredible people and they all explain in many ways similar philosophies to what I am about to share with you here. So this is my way, just one way of many, and maybe, just maybe, it will be of service to you. This is my interpretation of ancient teachings. There is nothing new here, only a sharing of ancient wisdom as I have understood it.

My Law – Tieme Ranapili

The sun may be clouded, yet ever the sun
Will sweep on its course till the cycle is run
And when into chaos the system is hurled
Again shall the builder reshape a new world
Your path may be clouded uncertain your goal
Move on for your orbit is fixed to your soul
And though it may lead into darkness of night
The torch of the builder shall give it new light
Your were, you will be know this while you are
Your spirit has travelled both long and afar
It came from the source, to the source it returns
The spark, which was lighted eternally burns
It slept in a jewel. It leapt in a wave
It roamed in the forest. It rose from the grave
It took on strange garbs for long eons of years
And now in the soul of your self it appears
From body to body your spirit speeds on
It seeks a new form when the old one has gone
And the form that it finds is the fabric you wrought
On the loom of the mind from the fibre of thought
As dew is drawn upwards, in rain to descend
Your thoughts drift away and in destiny blend
You cannot escape them, for petty or great
Or evil or noble, they fashion your fate
Somewhere on some planet, sometime and somehow
Your life will reflect your thoughts of your now
My law is unerring. No blood can atone
The structure you built you will live in alone
From cycle to cycle, through time and through space

Your lives with your longings will ever keep pace
And all that you ask for, all you desire
Must come at your bidding as flame out of fire
Once list to that voice and all that is done
Your life is the life of the infinite one
In hurrying race you are conscious of pause
With love for the purpose and love for the cause
Your are your own Devil, you are your own God
You fashioned the paths your footsteps have trod
And no one can save you from error or sin
Until you have harked to the spirit within.

(attributed to a Maori)

Contents

Introduction

My name is Nicky. I am slightly bonkers. I have a wonderful family and amazing friends and a life that I am truly grateful for.

At the ripe old age of forty-eight, four years after starting this book I am again beginning at the beginning. I want this book to be of service to you, even if it is in the smallest way. I want the wisdom that I have learned to reach you, to empower you to make shifts in your own life.

Everything I share has been written about countless times by some extraordinary people whose wisdom and knowledge is both fascinating and beautiful.

It was the face and words of a participant in a recent workshop that made me get my act together and start revamping what I have written and rewritten many times. 'Why don't we know this stuff?'

It is a great question and the answer is we do, it is just buried so deeply within us that we have forgotten. We have to wake up and stay awake. We have to raise our awareness and to do this we have to know how.

Chapter 1

More Than a Trend

This book is about shamanism and before you put it down, I encourage you to take a moment to consider why you picked this book up in the first place. You see this book knows you are looking for answers and maybe, just maybe you will find some right here.

The word 'shaman' is open to much misperception and judgment simply because of misunderstanding and perhaps because of the way shaman men and women have been portrayed in the past. The philosophy and practice is the oldest known to mankind. Shamanism is very deeply connected to the rhythm of all of life and dates back earlier than most religions, to a time when our ancestors understood the participatory connection we have with everything we are surrounded by.

In the dictionary it states a shaman is the person who can contact good and evil spirits. This is an interesting definition. The shaman I have met see the universe as benign and the existence of only heavy and light energy. They see from their hearts into hidden realms. They are aware that good and evil only exists in the hearts and minds of men and women. They remember a way of stepping between the world of energy and the world that we know. They recognize the potential in a person to sustain harmony rather than dwell in their past. A shaman uses their ability to be of service to another by empowering another to adjust their energetic vibration and therefore their physical life and the direction that they are heading.

Value in Times of Change

The purpose of this book is to describe and illustrate the wisdom of the shaman, what the knowledge can be used for, when and how it can be used to assist us in daily life. What I share is only a fraction of the wisdom available to us through the teachings of the shamanic ways.

The reality is that there are no quick fixes. However, using the knowledge and the tools passed down to us we can shift our lives by first shifting our very own energy field. Yes, we still have decisions and choices to make and these come more naturally and more gracefully when we can apply the wisdom in our own lives. It is a journey that demands dedication and commitment and when used and applied and practiced regularly it delivers astonishing shifts. You will begin to recognize the enormous value and potential of applying this wisdom in your life.

Change is the only constant and yet most of us fear change. Most of us prefer to stay with what we know even if it is not working very well, is hurting us and is unsustainable. Whilst change is inevitable we tend towards resistance purely because we are afraid of what the changes will mean. We prefer to stay with the comfort of our discomfort. The awareness and tools of the shaman assist us to adapt more quickly and to become more flexible to the notion that change happens. As I am writing this book we are experiencing extreme changes in climate and in our social systems that after a century of coping with the demands placed upon them are beginning to break down. This happens in our personal worlds and within our bodies if we do not adapt.

The awareness and the philosophy of the shaman can assist us to find stability even when things around us are uncertain and appear unstable. The knowledge and wisdom supports us, empowering us to look beyond our worries and our fears, enabling us to move away from systems that are not working. They help us to create our own new maps, and our own new systems from a new place, a place of cooperation and in a way that is sustainable.

Origins

There are a number of shamanic philosophies originating from different regions of the world, just as there are religions and other practices like mindfulness, NLP, meditation and yoga etc. All these different pathways are often communicating the same thing only in a different language and depending where we are in our lives will depend upon the language that we will resonate with.

The knowledge that I share from in this book originates from the wise men and women in the high Andes who, up until the mid-20th century, had remained relatively unknown, as had the philosophy of shamanism. This body of knowledge has been cherished and shared by the descendants of the Laika and Inca, the Q'ero nation, who fled well above the tree line into the mountains during the invasion of South America by the Spanish conquistadors. They had foreseen in their own prophecies that men with sticks of fire would arrive and they took the action to maintain and safeguard the teachings of this philosophy that stretch back over five thousand years.

Living well above the tree line in the mountain landscapes of Peru, the Q'ero nation continues to practice and share their knowledge with each generation, ensuring its survival. With no influence from religion or science it remains as pure today as it has always been. The difference today is that science is finally beginning to catch up and through the discovery of quantum physics we are now realizing the potential of this wisdom to assist us all through times of great change.

It remains a body of wisdom that embraces all other philosophies, for it is based in the pure energy and elements that make up all of life and that are essential to the continuation of life on this amazing and formidable planet. I want to make clear that this is not the only way, but one way of many. The teachings are experiential because unless we experience something for ourselves we cannot know if it works for us. This is a body of experiential knowledge, empowering us to make the shifts in our lives that are required to maintain and sustain a balanced way of living. A body of knowledge that provides us with the tools to recognize we do have the power within us to change the way we experience the life we find ourselves living and that we have a participatory role in the world. A world where we are all connected through a web of energy, which we influence and are influenced by.

As we begin to walk this path we experience the subtle and deep ways in which we really do influence and participate in our world. We begin to raise our awareness and we wake up. And once we are awake living our lives with our eyes open, we become more conscious of what we are creating and life becomes part of an incredible journey. We never want to fall asleep in our lives again.

This is a path of fire, for shaman recognise that we are all light vibrating at a different resonance and that this creates matter into different forms like humans, animals, plants and oceans. If light is bound into matter, then light can be unbound, just as we unbind the sun from wood to make fire. Just as in physics it is stated that energy cannot be born or extinguished, it purely changes form. Therefore it exists everywhere in all that we recognize as our world and all that remains unseen in our world.

Alberto Villoldo studied for over twenty-five years with the Q'ero shaman and continues to work with the Q'ero and other shaman. His journey began through his interest in the mind and his studies as an anthropologist. Alberto has written many books and I would recommend them to any of you who may be interested in delving further into this path.

During his research Alberto met Don Antonio Morales and together they journeyed and created the methods now shared through the Four Winds Society training. The difference is the language used to share the knowledge. Don Antonio Morales knew through the prophesies of his people that the generations of shaman to come would be of the West and so the partnership between Alberto and Antonio provided a way for this incredible knowledge to be shared in a language that you and I can understand.

My journey with Alberto and Linda Fitch, then CEO of the Society, pushed me well outside of any comfort zone I had and liberated me so that I was able to take the opportunity to teach and share this wisdom on behalf of the Four Winds Society. It has been and continues to be an incredible journey. After moving to France and exploring a new culture and language it is time to step again into the place of sharing this wisdom and most importantly how we can apply this in our everyday lives.

What Science Says

We have a relationship with all of creation and we are here as caretakers to ensure the continuation of the evolution of life on planet earth. Shaman cannot understand our ideas that we were cast out of the Garden or that the force that created everything we know lives somewhere else. They experience the organizing principles of creation as existing in everything we know and everything we do not know. They have always known that the world of matter and the world of energy are directly interlinked.

Many years ago, actually hundreds of years ago, we gave the job of working out why we are here and our place and purpose to the created research called science. Throughout evolution our ancestors, just like us, had to face the difficult task of unpicking belief systems that had been held as true when a huge leap of knowledge highlighted that perhaps what we held as true might not be as true as we once thought.

Shaman say every belief is limiting and a self-fulfilling prophecy. Beliefs are created through perception and perception is a learned phenomena. Understanding this on a deep level assists us to shift our perception and as this occurs on the inside our beliefs, actions, habits and values shift as well. And as our internal world shifts so our experience of the world we perceive on the outside follows.

Up until the 20th century we had been, and still are to an extent, influenced by the observations and perception of Charles Darwin, who stated that in the natural world 'only the strongest survive.' Interestingly this mythology still silently informs us even though science has come on leaps and bounds in its understanding of how the universe works and our place within it. If we look at this old mythology we can perhaps see why we live in a society that bases itself on a set of criteria run by fear, fighting battles and wars. Even before Darwin we can see mythologies based on fear throughout human existence. However, this latest scientific observation anchored itself into society so influencing our beliefs. It introduced a hierarchy system into our experiences of life. Wise men and women have always known that the universe and the natural world exists by way of community, cooperation, help and sustainability as opposed to our systems of individualism, competition, fear and fighting.

Thankfully science has begun to catch up with the knowledge of our ancestors. In 1944 a physicist, Max Planck, presented a lecture where he made a statement that shocked the scientific world of the time. He confirmed that through his research of matter and atoms he concluded that there was no matter. That all matter existed because of a force that brings particles of atoms to a particular vibration and holds it together in form. He stated that we must assume the existence of a conscious and intelligent force, which he called the matrix of all matter.

He identified the very field that our ancestors knew of over five thousand years ago. Through Max Planck's studies science can now confirm the existence of a subtle energy field that connects everything in creation. Nothing is excluded. It is the universe within us and outside of us. This field of energy is the bridge between all that is possible in our mind and hearts and what becomes real in the world. Known as quantum physics, science has now confirmed that quantum particles remain connected and respond to each other even when separated by thousands of miles. That this subtle all inclusive energy field is holographic and so any part of the field contains everything in the field of energy, that the past, present and future merge with each other. This explains beautifully the knowledge of the shaman that there is no time or space. So for example when the shaman do the reading of the prophecies they are already tapping into the future and have been doing so since before time began. So whether we look at this from the perspective of science, religion or the shaman, it is clear that a force does exist that connects us all.

Then around 1950 there was the introduction of cardio-neurology, which confirmed the power of the heart to influence our world. Research found that the same neurons that operate in the brain exist in the heart and other major organs. There are about forty thousand neurons in the heart and these decode the messages of how we are feeling and send electrical impulses to our brain, which then sends out whatever the heart is saying our body requires. It is an intricate and intimate relationship and together the brain and the heart communicate to create an inner system that is sustainable. The heart has a brain and a memory and works without us even stopping for a moment to consider what is necessary for our bodies to function. This is until the levels of imbalance become unsustainable and then we begin to notice something is not working so well. We get sick and this can be on a physical, mental, emotional or soul level.

Most of us are aware of the term 'gut instinct' and our heart is at the centre of our ability to be intuitive. Our heart has an intelligence and energetic power we are still discovering and understanding. The intelligence of our heart bypasses the filters that inform our brains. Our brain filters information through the mind, thinking based on past experiences, whereas the heart makes decisions on our wellbeing based in the moment. Scientific studies have shown that we make a judgment in as little as a tenth of a second and these initial impressions from our heart in the moment are often right on the button. However, in our society that discards intuition for the power of thinking we often convince ourselves that our intuition was out because we immediately pull in the brain/mind, which then thinks based on the past.

The Essence of Shamanism

The knowledge that the Q'ero cherish is made of simple maps that reflect the interconnected relationship we have with the world around us. The path is a path of empowerment that provides experiences from which we can begin to raise our awareness and become more awake in our life, recognizing the kind of world we are creating within and around us. The knowledge is a set of tools or experiences that are indispensable and can be utilized in our lives every day.

The very essence of this shamanic path is to create from the potential of an individual or situation in the moment, rather than creating from the past, which only serves to lead us into a repeat performance of a time gone by.

The ceremonies conducted by a shaman are in service of another who is experiencing disease. The feathers, drums and rattles are tools a shaman uses to reach a certain state of consciousness and awareness. Here at a different energetic vibration they can assist another human being release heavy (negative) energy from their energy body, which in turn releases everything associated with this from the physical body and mind. The shaman knows that making a shift in our energy body directly informs our whole being, so enabling harmony to be restored.

Chapter 2

How the Shaman Sees the Body's Energy Field

We are here to grow rainbow bodies. The energy field around our physical body is connected to our physical body by what is commonly known as the chakra system. The shaman knows these as whirlpools of light and each one vibrates radiating colour.

The word chakra comes from a Sanskrit word meaning 'wheel' – translated a chakra is a wheel of light. A chakra is like a powerhouse of energy, a bit like a battery and we have seven associated with our physical body and the shaman talk of two that sit outside our physical body; one that rests within our energy field known as the eighth chakra or source of the sacred and one that rests outside known as the ninth chakra connected to the cosmos. They are charged and recharged through their connection with our own energy field and the matrix of energy of the cosmos. This energy source is always available and free, unlike the electricity supply to our homes.

We have a vertical power strip that runs from the top of our head to the base of our spine. The spine holds our nervous system highway communicating and relaying information throughout our physical body. Our seven major chakras are aligned with our spine. They maintain and regulate the flow of energy throughout our electrical network within our physical body, spinning clockwise at a regular speed providing energy ready to be used when needed. Our chakra system is the interface between our energy body and our physical body and our experience of life.

Our chakras are sensitive to changes in energy and can become sluggish and clogged for many reasons from our mental and emotional state to the condition of our energy field. When our body's energy system cannot flow then we are susceptible to imbalance or disease.

There are many books on chakras available; there is a brief map of the chakras to follow, but first I want you to take a look at your chakras based on now.

So take a deep breath in, close your eyes and focus your attention on your first or base chakra. Get a sense of your chakra, what do you sense, you can hold your hand over the pubic bone to help focus your attention.

Is there a colour?

A sound?

A feeling?

Note these down. Does the energy feel sluggish or do you get the sense the energy is potential waiting to be utilized?

Repeat this exercise for each chakra, so from your first chakra you take your attention up to your second chakra, which is about two inches down from your belly button. Follow the same map as above then take your attention to your third chakra, found in-between your rib cage, a few inches up from your belly button, then up to your fourth chakra, located at the centre of your breastbone. Then your fifth chakra located at your throat. Then your sixth chakra located in-between and just above your eyebrows, and finally your seventh chakra at the top of your head.

Once you have this information noted down you can perhaps get a sense of your own chakras and maybe a picture of what they are telling you about your energy. If any feel sluggish or blocked then you can help discharge heavy energy by spinning each one individually counter or anti-clockwise imagining that you are pulling out heavy energy sitting in that wheel of light. You can do this just quietly sitting, giving the heavy energy to the earth or you can choose to do this standing in the shower with the water running cleansing each chakra like you are going up in a lift. As soon as you feel you have cleansed the chakra then spin the chakra clockwise again to complete the exercise before moving up to the next chakra. It is a simple exercise but very effective and useful as a self-maintenance programme easily integrated into the routine of the day.

What follows is a basic map of my understanding of the chakras.

Chakra 1 – known as the base or root chakra
Colour – red
Location - base of the spine between the anus and genitalia
Associated – earth and grounding, physical survival, our fight or flight response
Body – legs, feet, bones, large intestines and adrenal glands

Chakra 2 – known as sacral
Colour – orange
Location three fingers down from your belly button
Associated – self-identity, desire, pleasure, sexuality, procreation and creativity
Body – lower abdomen, kidneys, bladder, circulatory system, reproductive organs and glands.

Chakra 3 – known as solar plexus
Colour – yellow
Location – few inches above your belly button in-between the rib cage
Associated – seat of emotional life, personal power, laughter, joy, anger, sensitivity and ambition.
Body – digestive system, muscles, pancreas and adrenals

Chakra 4 – known as heart chakra or house of the soul
Colour – green
Location - centre of the breastbone around the level of the heart
Associated – love, compassion, harmony, peace, jealousy, envy
Body – lungs, heart, arms, hands and thymus gland

Chakra 5 – throat
Colour – turquoise
Location – throat
Associated – communication, creativity, self-expression, judgement, senses of inner and outer hearing
Body – neck, shoulders, arms, hands, thyroid and parathyroid

Chakra 6 – brow or third eye
Colour – indigo
Location – centre of your forehead slightly above eye level
Associated – questions re the spiritual nature of life, perception and knowing, inner vision, intuition and wisdom, denial, depression and delusion
Body – brain, eyes, nervous system and pituitary gland

Chakra 7 – crown chakra
Colour – violet
Located – top of head
Associated – selflessness, integrity, acceptance, universal ethics, regression, cynicism and psychoses
Body – skin, brain, hormone balance, central nervous system and pineal gland

Chakra 8 – source of the sacred
Colour – gold
Located - a few inches above your head
Associated – transcendence, the architect of the physical body

Chakra 9 – infinity
Colour – translucent white light
Location – cosmos
Associated – liberation and infinity

We all have a ninth chakra but there is only one ninth chakra said to be the place of oneness, where we all recognize ourselves in each other, that we are all a representation of the same source from which all life is created.

Our energy field itself has different layers within it and each one of these layers is a source of energy for us on a physical, mental, emotional, soul and spiritual level. The quality of the energy and the condition of our energy field has a direct impact on us, and the life we experience. These levels are covered by a membrane just like our skin covers our internal organs and acts like a memory bank influencing the kind of life we live, our health, how we will age and how 'we may die'. It holds memories of events that have yet to be reconciled. Similar situations, or relationships activate the memory and this downloads the story including thoughts, words, beliefs, behaviours and values, which influence the life we experience. Many times we are not even consciously aware of the original event but we will continue to step into similar experiences until we can discharge the heavy energy that keeps this memory imprinted in our energy field. Often we can see no reason why we are suddenly behaving differently or adversely or we recognize a replay of an old pattern but do not know how to step beyond it. Another trigger can be an event that is highly charged with negative emotions which, if held on to, can create a memory which scores our energy field just like the grooves on a record. This then sits in our energy field until we replay the event through another situation in an effort to reconcile and release the heavy energy we are holding on to.

If we are awake enough to make the shift by honouring the situation in the moment, discharging the heavy energy through our chakras, then our vibration becomes lighter and with the reconciliation comes the ability to step beyond the past taking only the wisdom we have gained with us creating the possibility of something new in our life. If we find ourselves in a challenging situation and reconciliation occurs instantaneously no groove is cut so no memory is held. For example, if we have no groove in our energy field for illness, if or when we do get sick we recover quickly. The reason is that these grooves or memories in our energy field act like magnets and unless we can reconcile and discharge the heavy energy they will just keep reorganizing and creating circumstances that seem slightly different but that are effectively a replay of the past in an effort for us to come to a place of reconciliation within. With reconciliation and a lightening of our energy field comes a new level of health and wellbeing. We move beyond the old vibration, the old pattern, and are available for a different experience.

Let us take surgery. If we have an operation to remove a lump, an organ or to clear a blockage in our blood vessels, unless we recognize the deeper message our body is giving us and through honouring release the anchor that holds this energy in place, the likelihood is that this will manifest again perhaps in a different place looking slightly different but the reason for the manifestation is still informing our body and our life.

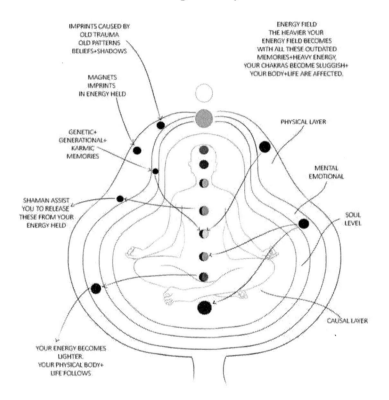

Because our energy field is like an archive we can find etchings or memories that come from former lifetimes or from the family line we have been born into. Basically any business left unfinished stays in our energy field and the shaman say that when we die our chakras disengage and our energy field collapses, passing through a hole the size of a molecule taking anything remaining with it so as we create a new body these same areas of heavy or un-reconciled energy turn up and we encounter more of the same. It makes sense to clear our energy field, reconcile our differences, clear the heavy sludgy energy through our chakras and grow a translucent rainbow body. That way we do not leave any outstanding legacy for our children to reconcile and when creating a new body we can begin to live truly in the moment. And the positive thing is that it is possible to do this now, this lifetime.

Sometimes we are really not aware of what is encoded into our energy. In this lifetime we have no memory of another life and rarely do we have a clear memory of events that happened to us when we were very small. In fact most of our memory of events is what we made it mean rather than a clear short version of what actually happened. Our energy system records the details and banks the heavy energy. We create a strategy to survive the life we knew and forty years down the line we are still living and surviving in the same way.

Whatever roles we play in our life these teachings simply remind each and every one of us that we are all a representation of a core life force manifesting itself in a form we know as ourselves. Through the teachings we learn that we are all special and we all have a purpose. We are all a representation of the evolution of humankind. With every generation within a family, society or culture comes the opportunity to reconcile and evolve past patterns, beliefs, behaviours and values. In the world of the shaman we realize that nothing is ever personal and we recognize that there is always a much greater picture. Maybe we cannot see it or maybe we are not totally aware of it but we know that we are part of a dynamic, a set of circumstances created so that an opportunity can arise to learn more about ourselves. We do not have to use feathers, drums and rattles to live a fulfilling and authentic life.

The shaman aspires to walk softly on the earth leaving no tracks. Translated this means that we own what is ours, we honour and step beyond that which no longer serves us and I am not talking about our material possessions. I am talking about owning every aspect of ourselves, reconciling our differences on the inside, becoming aware of the stories that run us, of the patterns we have inherited, or the beliefs we have created and the lives we find ourselves living.

What Does Spiritual Mean?

This wisdom is not new; it exists in every one of us, we have just buried it so deep we have to have tools to rediscover what we already know.

These teachings are like investing in a really good pair of walking boots. They support you even when the terrain is uncertain and help you find footholds when you need to climb what seem like mountains. In the same way they help you to explore your own inner garden so that you can have the courage to discover what you are cultivating. Our inner gardens are often neglected because we have become so consumed by our exterior physical world. When we begin to look sometimes the garden is overgrown. Plants we never knew existed have taken root.

We begin to look closely at the brambles, the unknown plants and the weeds and we see that beauty does exist even in something we perceive as ugly. In our inner garden we want to honour the beauty even when it is not pretty and then we clear the weeds and the brambles, giving them to the compost or the garden fire. The compost brings us nutrients to feed our garden and we begin to plant our own seeds, grow beautiful flowers, creating a garden for ourselves. Then we no longer spend our life waiting for someone to bring us flowers and we stop blaming others because we don't have any. A path of empowerment to create an extraordinary garden is the promise of something beautiful for those yet to come.

This is my interpretation of spiritual and for me the very essence of what it means to live authentically following the shamanic way. An inner journey recognizing ourselves in all things knowing that what we experience is created within us.

A spiritual path is an extraordinary journey that we embark upon back to our essential selves. My mum shared with me her thoughts in the weeks before she passed away. We were talking about faith, religion and beliefs.

Mum said, "Even if we both believed in God, your experience and my experience of God would be different. We could read the same words, follow the same practices but we all have our own personal experience, our own relationship with whatever faith, belief or religion we choose to follow. It cannot be the same relationship as anyone else. It is more about how we live our lives whilst we are here, the relationships we create and whether we become self- consumed or recognize ourselves in everyone doing our best to create balanced relationships that can be sustained. Our personal relationship with whatever we choose to call the life force that exists everywhere is not something we can have or hold. It simply exists and we somehow know of its existence."

Chapter 3

The Path of the Shaman

Your beliefs become your thoughts
Your thoughts become your words
Your words become your actions
Your actions become your habits
Your habits become your values
Your values become your destiny

Mahatma Gandhi

The shamanic path is a map containing wisdom that applied through experience becomes knowledge. It is not another book full of information. We cannot read how to be a better person or look online to find out how to change our life. We have tools that we have had experience of that through the experience provide us with the knowledge and support we require to navigate our way through our lives and the world we find ourselves living in.

You see, these days everyone expects a quick answer. Type the question into your computer and it gives you an answer. It all seems so easy until you then go to apply it in your life. For example my son wants to learn to drive. So we began to go out in the car, driving around the car park so he could get some experience of clutch control. About the third time we went out, nothing went right. He got so frustrated and I was really concerned about my clutch wear especially when it began to smell. Then my son said that when he had looked on the computer how to drive it had looked so easy and the tips he had taken from what he had watched he was now applying and they were not working. So we had a conversation that driving is really something you have to learn from experience, you cannot learn to drive by looking it up on the computer.

The technological era that we are all a part of has the potential to serve us in many ways and like all things it has the potential to create chaos; it all depends on how we choose to use it or how much we possess it. The shaman knows that anything we feel we have to possess will eventually possess us. We want to wake up to the fact that we are already giving ourselves over to technology, depending on our mobile phones and computers for the answers to many things in life; giving our personal data over in order to become part of a communication network for services. It works, yes, but there needs to be a balance. Take the time to reflect on your decisions, look at how much time you spend on your phone or computer. Use it yes for your endeavours but as the shaman says do not allow yourself to be used by technology. As human beings we want to know how to use our instincts and to know ourselves on the inside. There is a place for everything; it is what and how we create from the tools we have that makes the difference in the sustainability and longevity of our global community.

So this is the path, an experiential path that once the tools are anchored in just like when we learn to drive, the process comes naturally and we apply the skills and knowledge when we need to in our daily lives. The path is a challenging one. We are encouraged to look at the story we are telling about ourselves, how much of this story is held in patterns, beliefs and behaviours that come from the past. It gets us to look at the roles that we play in our life and our expectations of ourselves in these roles and our perception of the expectations of others. The path brings into our conscious awareness what is really driving the momentum and direction we are heading in. The knowledge in the teachings provides us with simple tools to help us shift old outmoded ways of being in our lives and ultimately gives us the opportunity to show up for our life right now rather than continuing to move forward into the past. In making a commitment to ourselves to make the difference we are shifting energy that in turn influences a dynamic far greater than we can possibly imagine.

Tools of the Shaman

Opening Sacred Space

Shamans always begin their work by opening sacred space. In this space we leave behind all the affairs of ordinary life and prepare to hold a place of sacredness for another. This space is not serious or ponderous. Shamans take their work seriously, and themselves lightly. There is often laughter and playfulness. Within sacred space we experience the lightness of our being.

The opening prayer is from the Q'ero tradition, there are others relating to different traditions, however the intention of each is the same.

The prayer encompasses our spatial directions. We call upon the four cardinal points of the compass, earth, heaven and the shaman (this is anyone of us). Science knows the four organizing principles of the universe as

Strong nuclear force
Weak nuclear force
Gravity
Electromagnetism

As shamans we know them as
South – Serpent – binding principle, the place of matter the material world
West – Jaguar – the renewing force, bringing order from chaos, mulching
North – Hummingbird – the epic journey of evolution and growth
East – Eagle /Condor – self transcending principle
Earth – Pachamama – receptive force
Heaven – Great Spirit – creative force
And the shaman. (individual opening the space).

These are known as the seven organizing principles of the universe. And when you call these principles in you align yourself with the forces that animate all of life. In sacred space the universe conspires on our behalf. We are no longer the performer but the channel through which these energies can be utilized, always in service of another, to empower another to do what they need to, to live their life fully to meet their spirit with passion and inspiration. The shaman will never fix anything, or control anything or try to gain power over another. The shaman chooses the path of service and empowerment.

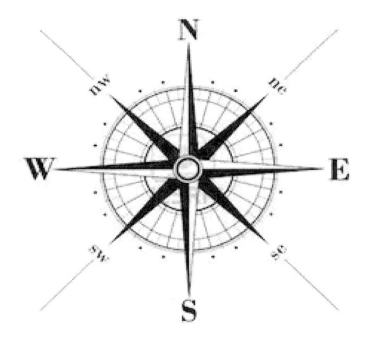

Opening Prayer

The call to the directions comes from the heart, it is the voice of love.

The prayer is used both at the beginning and the end of our ceremony or work. By closing, acknowledging and thanking the directions, the archetypical energies we have called reintegrate into nature. The prayer can encompass elements that are personal to you. With a pure intention and the calling of the directions the energy of a safe and empowering space is created.

This prayer is my interpretation of the prayer used by Alberto Villoldo. You will discover your own prayer as prayer itself morphs depending on the situation. So be available to discover your own prayer.

OPENING SACRED SPACE—THE MEDICINE WHEEL

THE INCA CROSS—CHAKANA

THE FOUR MOST IMPORTANT CORNER REPRESENTS
- THE CARDINAL DIRECTIONS
- THE FOUR ELEMENTS
  EARTH, WATER, FIRE, AIR
- THE FOUR BIG STARS IN THE SOUTHERN CROSS

To the sacred winds of the South, Great Serpent
Come wrap your coils of light around us
Help us to shed our past the way that you shed your skin

Easily and effortlessly
That we may walk lightly and with beauty upon the earth.
Teach us how to walk leaving no tracks and no ripples through time or through space no business unfinished as a legacy for our children's children.

To the sacred winds of the West, mother sister jaguar
Come protect our medicine space,
You who have seen the birth and death of galaxies
Assist us to walk the rainbow bridge between the worlds.
Help us to walk as the luminous warrior with no enemies in this world or the next.
Teaching us to walk the way of peace and with impeccability.
Stepping beyond fear and beyond death that we may participate fully in life.

To the sacred winds of the North, Syri Kinti Royal Hummingbird.
Show us how to sip from the rich nectar of life and of knowledge
Bring us stillness in motion as we take our epic journey
Grandmothers, Grandfathers, ancient ones those of you who have stepped outside of time, we welcome you, come warm your hands by our fire.
Whisper to us on the wind that we may hear your wisdom.
We honour you all, those who have come before us, and all those who will come after us, our children's children.

To the sacred winds of the East
Great Eagle, Great Condor
Come to us from the place of the rising sun
Take us under your wings that we may fly above the mountains with spirit.
Bring us your gracefulness in flight, so that we may see from our hearts with vision and clarity
That we may fly wingtip to wingtip with the Great Spirit.

Pachamama, sacred Mother Earth
The mother who never leaves us
We come in service of all your children
The stone people, the plant people, the four-legged, the two-legged, the many-legged, the winged, the finned and the furred ones. All our relations.

Father Sun for light life and the courage in our hearts to live life fully. Grandmother moon and the sacred star nations for always watching over us, lighting the sky when it is dark, guiding us in dream time and reminding us of our origins, that we are all made of star dust.

Great Spirit you who are known by many names and yet remain nameless.
For this incredible song of creation, we give thanks that we are gathered here to sing the song of life for one more day. HO!

These prayers coupled with our intention set our focus and align us so that we step into a place of service. Ultimately we become available to be in a place to empower another to see opportunity and possibility in their life.

I remember during my own training many years ago, we were working as a group and one of the guys was closing space after our group work was completed. It went like this.

Serpent salt of the earth, cheers mate
Jaguar, you're a diamond
Hummingbird, great job
Eagle, stunning mate

We were all laughing and looking at each other, thinking well that's not how the closing prayer is supposed to sound. What it was, was authentic and came from the man's heart. He really meant it and this is what is important. What a great lesson for all of us so intent on doing it the right way.

The Wiracocha (Source of the Sacred)

We also have our own sacred space, known as WIRACOCHA meaning source of the sacred in the Quechan language. When we open our own sacred wiracocha it enables our own energy field to expand outwards just as it does when in nature and open spaces. It is a place in which we can pause to get a sense of our own energy.

It is a source that we can utilize whenever we feel we require a safe quiet space. To open your wiracocha, you reach your hands up above your head and imagine there is a golden ball of light, just like the sun. Take a moment to feel and experience this. How and what do you experience?

Then take your hands and, as if moving them up and through the centre of your wiracocha, open this luminous ball of light down and around you. Just like the sun's rays as they come up over the horizon at the dawn of a new day.

Experience for yourself this space of quiet and calm. If you are saying to yourself I feel nothing, then imagine what it would feel like. If you were to experience something what might it be? What might it look like? Sound like? What colour? What vibration? Use your imagination. As you open your eighth chakra around you, your luminous energy field begins to expand towards the edges of this cocoon, just like when we are in nature.

This is the space where you can leave the affairs of ordinary life and experience the synchronicity and wonder of the world of energy. Where you can get to experience your own energy field vibration and do what is necessary to maintain it.

So for example if you feel like there is a gap or hole in your energy field then repair it however you feel it needs repairing. Let the freedom of your imagination guide you. It is our imagination that is the key that allows us to open the doors when we can find no way through logically. Our imagination helps us to create images so we begin to see, hear and feel from a different place. Even if you do this much for two minutes a day you are giving yourself two minutes of high vibe space, a moment to pause. Remember it does not need to be a huge amazing long-drawn-out affair to be significant. A couple of minutes can make all the difference to the flow of your day.

There have been many situations in my life when, merely by opening sacred space, even if it has been silently in my head, incredible shifts have occurred or the moment of high vibe space helps someone feel safe enough to explore something that perhaps they have never felt they could.

When we open sacred space, there is no opinion, no judgment, no expectation and no performer. What we have is a stillness that invites us to get to know ourselves truly and it allows a space for others to do the same.

It is like providing a witness, like the great trees and the mountains. They listen and provide a space for us to answer our own questions, honour our own demons and begin to participate in creating our lives.

The Levels of Engagement

The levels of engagement are a useful shamanic way of looking at how we communicate every day. It has been said that any situation that arises whether we deem it good or bad cannot be resolved at the same level of engagement that it was created.

In these teachings we have already talked about the four cardinal points that hold sacred space for us in the ecosphere. Serpent, Jaguar, Hummingbird and Eagle represent these.

We attribute these same archetypes to each of the levels of engagement through association with the chakra system. And curiously we have a brain that corresponds with each.

The first level of engagement is the literal, represented by serpent at our first chakra. The corresponding part of the human brain is the reptilian brain.

The reptilian brain regulates our systems on a cellular level and our autonomic functions like breathing. We do not have to think about breathing; but did you know dolphins have to choose to breathe, when they go to sleep only one side of their brain sleeps whilst the other side helps them to remember to breathe.

This is the place of the cold hard facts, black and white, what you see is what you see. At this level there is no emotion. It is purely instinctive, no drama, do or say what needs to be in the moment. This is the doctor in accident and emergency who knows exactly what needs to be done and does it. If the doctor is in the level of engagement of emotions, then I may not make it, because emotions can affect the way in which we operate. If we get too emotional we cannot think straight. This is why in panic we often make mistakes.

The second level of engagement is the symbolic, represented by Jaguar at our second chakra. The corresponding part of the human brain is the mammalian or limbic brain. This brain has programs we share with all animals; fear, fighting, feeding and sex. This brain also understands ritual and ceremony and is where our early defences against perceived enemies derived and created human superstition.

Here is the level of emotion, where nothing is as it seems. So you see colours, let's say white yellow and green in a shape that is a flower. This is where you meet a guy covered in tattoos only to find he is a religious leader. Not what you might expect.

At this level of engagement we have emotion, we have drama, we have feelings. This is where we as human beings spend a lot of our time. So it stands to reason that a number of issues that arise come from this level of engagement.

An example. I was engaged in an argument with my teenage son about homework. He could not be bothered and was irritated at having to do the work. He asked for my help but didn't really want it. I became irritated, he became more irritated and angry and so did I. Then surprisingly enough the whole situation exploded. We were getting nowhere. So I stopped and changed the level at which I was engaging with him and asked him if he could see what was happening. He could, of course, and verified that we were both getting more and more angry. So I offered that we start again and asked him exactly what it was that he had to do. He replied and so I said, "Okay, let's do just that." And we did, no more drama, no more emotion. What a relief. I had woken up to what was happening and shifted the level out of the emotional down if you like to the level of serpent where we look from the eyes of black and white, no emotion. It takes practice but is so valuable in our lives. The ability to change the way in which we communicated enabled us to get on with what needed to be accomplished and still be friends at the end.

The third level of engagement is the mythic represented by hummingbird and associated with the third chakra, the solar plexus. The corresponding part of the human brain is the neocortex. This is the brain that evolved logic and creativity. In a hundred thousand years there was a quantum leap in the evolution of the brain but it was only visionaries that knew how to use it, like the great philosophers and mathematicians. This is the place of images, of poetry, of yes, believe it or not, maths, of symbols and dreams. This is the place of fairy tales, and many important moral stories regarding human life and the journey we take are told through myth and fairy tales.

Here is where we can open ourselves up to receive insight into situations in our lives. Just as we do when we are in the South direction looking at the stories we tell of ourselves, we also take this to the realm of imagination where we see our life as a river. Taking our level of engagement up to this level can help us to see things that perhaps would go unnoticed at the level of the physical and emotional.

The fourth level of engagement is that of spirit, represented by Eagle, and is associated with the fourth chakra, the heart chakra. The corresponding part of the human brain is the prefrontal lobe also known as the God brain. This is the brain that comes on line during meditation and has been witnessed by experiments with Buddhist monks who had scans during their enlightenment activities. Only the prefrontal, God brain was active during these moments.

Here the level of engagement is purely energetic. Here we can touch a sense of nothing, of pure energy where there are no limits and where we recognize that we are a part of the whole. We use this level of engagement to work as a shaman, for here we are working ninety-nine percent energy and one percent matter. And it is far easier to shift things whilst they are in the realm of energy than when they have manifested in the physical and material world. That does not mean that we can just give stuff up to spirit. We take the responsibility to discern what it is that is of service and how we will share that before we let the vision or the image go back to the energetic realm.

Never do we work from a place of 'well spirit told me it was ok' or in the name of spirit I do this. Spirit or the universe is benign; it purely responds to our demands. This is why as shaman we must clear up our own back yards and be very clear about our responsibility to use right thought, right heart and right action. No commands are given by spirit. It is our discernment that counts. Our integrity. So if you find yourself in a situation that is maybe uncomfortable and let's face it they happen, this is life after all. Be aware and awake. At what level of engagement did this situation begin? How can you shift the level of engagement and approach things differently?

It may still be uncomfortable, but there may be a greater chance of an outcome that is genuinely of service to all those involved whether it is deemed good or bad. A deep understanding of how this works is an essential part of the shamanic training, as from here, the shaman learns how to raise this knowledge to the perceptual states or shaman's way of seeing.

After many years creating my own relationship with the teachings I am human and I must tell you that I do forget. Yep even after all I have learned, I am forever a student of life and when I am in the thick of my own personal life, I sometimes forget everything that is available to me. You see I am not just a shaman, I play many roles like Mum, wife, friend, colleague to name a few and this keeps me real, compassionate, forgiving and able to hold a space for another because I remember that we are being human and life happens. The encounters keep coming until we get it and to get it, we have to be consciously awake and aware of ourselves, of our interior world, our interior voices because we are the only person who has direct access to these. For many reasons we can dress them up to look like other things when we present them to the world. You know when you book an appointment to see someone and you arrive with your issue only to establish that it is actually something much deeper. I have done this on more than one occasion and in order to do this takes courage because we have to take a good look at ourselves without any of our disguises.

Remember we are all energy vibrating, so I hope it makes sense when I say we were never meant to carry heavy energy, it lowers our vibration. Like a baby or small child the energy of experience creates feelings and these pass through us. A baby cries, and then one minute later the baby is laughing. The child gets angry, the next five minutes playing happily. The feelings come and go. As we get older we begin to make these experiences mean something about us turning them into emotions that for some reason we must shove in a bag and hang onto.

This stuff starts as energy but the longer we hold onto it, the more we hold onto it, the more heavy it becomes, starting in our energy field then clogging up our chakras and then sometimes manifesting in the physical body. If you do not let this energy pass through, it gets heavier and denser. It is a lot easier to shift something whilst it is still energy than when it becomes manifested physically. So here is a simple method to help release heavy or strong emotions.

Nature Painting

A nature painting comes from the Q'ero tradition. In the mountains of Peru the shamans use earth or sand mainly because there are no trees in the highlands in Peru and for this reason the shaman know this as a sand painting. We call it a nature painting because we have the good fortune to have more choice in what we can use to create this wonderful tool.

Legend and lore says that the creation of a sand painting is where we communicate with our spirit and where our spirit voice has the opportunity to work and speak through the natural world. So the nature painting is a place where we work our stuff in the realm of the mythic and energetic.

The nature painting is where we can begin to read the signs of the natural world, how to transpose them into our everyday lives and how this can assist us to make very subtle and yet powerful shifts in our experience of the everyday. It is a picture, a picture of us created in a circle that can be viewed from different places enabling us to look and see things differently.

First you are going to create sacred space by calling in the four directions, earth and spirit. You can use the prayer earlier or create your own.

Now here step by step is how to create your own nature painting.

1- You want to create a circle. The size is entirely up to you but I would suggest that you allow for at least the size of a large dinner plate. You can use twigs, leaves, and flowers. Whatever you feel you want to create the circle with is ok. I would suggest you keep the objects as natural as possible. Find one object to represent you, blow into this and place in the centre of the circle.

2- Find objects from nature to represent aspects of the issue or situation you're facing.

3- Take a deep breath and focus your attention inside of yourself; find the emotion, thoughts, beliefs or energy that you are holding within you that relates to the situation etc. Pull up the energy with your breath and blow onto the item you have chosen to represent this aspect. Then place each item into your circle. Be aware that you may have emotions or thoughts come up that you were not expecting, put it all in the nature painting.

4- You may have discomfort in your body. Again blow the energy into the object and place it where you feel it wants to go.

5- Take your time with this, allow yourself to be creative and stop thinking. Your mind is busy because you are doing something; allow the feelings to come up and your nature painting will create itself.

6- Spend a few moments with your circle; notice how you feel inside. Close your eyes, take a few deep breaths, open your eyes, notice what you are experiencing. If there appears to be nothing take the time to be with nothing and observe what this means for you.

7- You can take the time to walk around your nature painting, observing it from the four directions. From the ground, from above. Notice any change in how you feel depending on which position you view this creation. You are practicing a shift in perception.

8- Sacred space can remain open for as long as you leave your nature painting with the natural world. Once you feel it is complete then you can close sacred space, taking the time to thank each of the directions.

9- A nature painting can be left for a few days and during this time you can go back, take a look, move things if you feel you want to. Or you may find that things have been moved anyway. Know that in this moving and shifting in the place of the mythic it will continue to inform your life. Know that it is much easier to shift things like this than to take your whole life and make the shifts physically and emotionally. Know that when you step in the natural world has heard your call and recognizes you have made a commitment to make a difference in your life. The natural world will also give you messages through your nature painting so if something happens to your circle stay awake to the message it is giving you. Overlay the encounter on your daily life and see what it is telling you. Maybe it is an opportunity to see something that until now has remained hidden.

10- We use nature paintings for many reasons. They give us the opportunity to find places of heavy emotion inside of us, release it with our breath into a natural object and let it work there energetically, rather than holding it inside of us. A place where you can release heavy energy in the form of thoughts, emotions and behaviours and let them work energetically. You still have to make decisions and take action but you will find that often the shifts occur so subtly that it can be a while before you actually notice things are different.

11- The nature painting is a great tool to use for all kinds of situations, whether they are work, family, friend-related, any number of reasons. You can use them with children, with businesses. It is a great way to see what is really going on. The important thing to remember is that the nature painting is about you and your relationship with the issue you may be working with. If you find yourself wanting to use it to change other people, take a very close look at yourself; somewhere you are blaming someone else for the situation you find yourself in and as hard as this may seem the only way you can shift anything is by shifting your own perception of the whole dynamic and this is a good place to start.

I remember once I created a nature painting around some personal work which involved being busy all the time, feeling exhausted and resentful. So I created my sacred circle and placed some objects inside to represent the issues that had showed up in my life. These objects included some nuts that I had placed in the centre to represent nourishment. I left my creation and went indoors. Within a few minutes there were two squirrels in my circle eating my nuts. At first I wanted to bang on the window, I felt angry that they were in my space and eating my nuts.

Then I stopped myself; of course they were helping me to see how I felt. I was feeding others and no one was feeding me, but of course nobody else could; it was I who was not feeding myself and as a result I was feeling resentful and empty. As I stood and watched, one of the squirrels took a nut and buried it for a rainy day. Again this was a message that I had to go deeper to nourish myself. My yearning was for some space to feed myself. I wanted to nourish that deeper part of me. I saw that the anger and resentment I felt towards others was actually my own anger at myself for never listening and that if I would just allow myself the nourishment I craved then I would have far more to share with others. That is when I committed myself to a yoga practice, which was realistic and I could manage in my everyday schedule. By giving myself time to do something that nourished me I was far more available for others. I have many amazing stories about nature paintings. They truly can bring us subtle and yet amazing insights and messages.

I remember once during a vision quest we sent the participants out to create a nature painting to set their intention for their vision quest. One of the participants came running in very distressed because a cow had done a huge poo right in the middle of her nature painting. Now she had chosen to create her nature painting in a cow field and spirit speaks to us in many ways. She understood what that big poo symbolized once she had calmed down and had the opportunity to reflect on the intention and purpose of her quest. She realized she had let herself become a doormat and felt trodden down. After the hours in her medicine circle she returned to her nature painting to find the sun had dried the poo and she was able to lift this off and offer it to the fire. A very symbolic moment for the insights she had gained during her quest.

I will provide you with an explanation of vision quest later in the book, with details of how you can create your own.

So go create a nature painting. Have the experience.

First set your intention and then follow the steps. People sometimes ask after they have made a nature painting, what do I do now? Well you keep the nature painting until you get a sense that the energy is no longer there. It is difficult to explain but have a go and you will know what I mean. The shifts can be really subtle, if your intention is clear and you stay awake and aware of the dynamic you are in, you will notice a difference. It may be the tiniest thing but being small can be very significant.

A sequence of photos showing an evolving nature painting. When we are thinking too much we want to take it to the mythic.

Here is a nature painting in action. You can see that you can use anything. Here I have some pegs creating my circle, a stone in the center to represent me, then items that I have blown the issue into. This is all about writing a synopsis for this book. I was thinking too much. So I took it to the mythic.

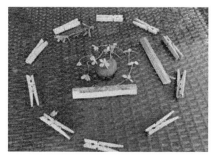

On the second day, when I returned to my nature painting, I felt like moving the items and this is what it looked like.

Afterwards, I sat and typed a synopsis and the wording flowed.

Day three when I arrived the circle had been moved and the flowers had moved. I moved one piece of wood.

Now I'm ready to send this synopsis with my book for consideration. Deep breath.

Treasure Maps

Another way that we can use the circle is in the way of a treasure map. This is a tool that I use after a vision quest but it can also be a useful way of looking at our life from the place of images, so again the level of engagement of the mythic. Often in this realm things reveal themselves that we would never have seen through thinking or talking about a situation. It is a great exercise to do with someone as the sharing of your images is often when the insight reveals itself.

So again the first thing is to set your intention. Take a white piece of paper and create a circle using a dinner plate or something bigger like a round tray. You will need scissors and glue. This exercise is done within thirty minutes otherwise you begin to think too much. This wants to be in the moment directed by your heart not your mind.

Then take a few magazines and flick through them very quickly; any images that jump out at you, cut them out and stick them on your circle. After the thirty minutes is up, stop. Stand back and look at your creation.

Get a sense of how it makes you feel and where you feel this in your body. Then share this with your partner. Whatever the insights are the use of this tool can be to call things in so you may want to keep the picture and hang it on your wall to remind you of the elements you are calling in or you can burn it if there are elements that you want to honour and release.

Having used this with clients it can often reveal shadow parts that have remained cleverly hidden but by bringing the situation into imagery they are revealed.

At the end of a vision quest the use and intention is very different and the treasure map is created to acknowledge the journey and the shift in a person's energy. To support this we come together surrounding the essence of the imagery in a bubble and we allow this to float up and out into the universe so into the realm of pure energy where there are no limitations and the dreams have the potential to manifest in ways far greater than we can imagine with our minds.

Both of these tools are fun to do and at the same time create a great opportunity for a shift in the way that we perceive our life. Have a go; we so rarely allow ourselves space to play, and by doing so we create a space for magic to occur.

Imagination, It Is the Key

Imagination holds a key. It is what fuels our dreams, it is where we spend our time as kids creating and dreaming. The energy comes from a place of spirit where everything and anything is possible.

Do you remember when you were a kid, how you imagined life to be, how you created games and played outside. How you imagined you could make life better, how you knew you could create whatever you wanted. Sadly as we grow older we realize that the world we live in is so full of rules and thinkers, that the imagination becomes something of a joke. You come up with an idea, which makes your heart sing, a call of your spirit, only to be told that it's not possible, what an earth were you thinking, get real!

Most of what we experience as real came from somebody's imagination; it was in this place that images and ideas came forth and were then taken by the thinker and put into action. Even Einstein said that before he would come up with a mathematical equation, first and foremost, he would get an image in his head and this would form into symbols and words. Where would music, poetry and art be without imagination? Really where would any of us be?

Back in our history and still in the native earth cultures of today they know that imagination and envisioning are the beginning of creating, of bringing something into reality. Just like the story of the Indian rain dance. Truly what we see is a process where the imagination brings envisioning and all the experiences one would have if it rained, for example. The ceremony is what the shaman or elders do to bring balance and to experience in feeling that their prayer is already happening.

Gregg Braden is another author I would recommend and his experience when he met with a Tibetan abbot explains this beautifully. He asked the abbot, "When we see your prayers, what are you doing? When we see the bells and the mantras on the outside what is happening to you on the inside?"

The abbot replied, "You have never seen our prayers, because prayer cannot be seen, what you have seen is what we do to create the feeling in our bodies. Feeling is the prayer!"

You have to create the feeling inside, to be peace inside if that is what you want to see outside in your world. Remember earlier I mentioned that the heart has a brain and that our heart brain informs our head brain what the body requires. It also has an energy that reaches much further than our physical body and scientific experiments have proved this to be true, but as yet the exact power of the energy of the heart remains unknown. Ancient teachings going way back through time have always endorsed the power of the heart and the shaman say that the balance inside requires an alignment of our heart, our thinking and our actions.

Mythic Mapping

Mythic mapping is how the shaman assists someone (a client) to create realistic coordinates in their everyday lives that help them to build and flourish in their new map of life.

We all of us have a map of life, determined by our experiences and what we have learned from our families and the societies that we live in. Remember our map of life is greatly influenced by others and sometimes by things we are not even consciously aware of.

After you have released heavy energy and the anchor of a belief system or way of behaving, the origin of the issue no longer exists and so you have an opportunity to step away from an old way of being, an old map of life and begin to create a new set of coordinates that support this.

After the process of release you have raised your energetic vibration and you are in a different place. You may feel completely different and want something new and different in your life. It is not always easy to imagine a new and different way of being if you have never experienced it before. And this is where mythic mapping comes in.

You have worked energetically. If we liken this to the levels of engagement you have worked in the realm of Eagle.

Now in this new place you are at the level of Hummingbird, the realm of the mythic, poetry, imagery, music and so on.

And before you go further remember the following:

- Stay awake
- Breathe
- Listen carefully
- Observe your body language
- Surrender to not having a clue

You have to stay awake as you have let go of something, your energy is different and now you are in a completely different place.

So become aware of your body and what you are experiencing, this gives you a thread to begin to work with. There may be an image or a sense of something that you cannot put into words. There may be a sound or a movement. Allow yourself time to find a way to express this new vibration. Allow yourself space to get used to this new way of being.

Then bring this into the realm of Jaguar by asking, what are the feelings inside your body? Where are they in the body? See if you can bring everything to a movement that anchors this new energy shift. Remember it takes about a month for our old behaviours to be overwritten so this is really important.

Then finally into Serpent – what can you bring into your life every day (that is realistic) to remind you of this new vibration and your new map.

Here it is important to ensure that what you decide is realistic. If you start with e.g. I will do an hour's yoga every day. You need to ask yourself: how am I going to do this, when and where in my everyday life?

Living the new map is every day so it may be simply a tiny movement that can be done anywhere, anytime without people asking questions. It is a tool for you to keep you in your new map. It may be a picture on the fridge door, a treasure map, a sand painting, a walk in the forest, touching a tree. It could be anything and here it is important that you find what works for you that is realistic.

It is not about what you think you should do. Be the shaman for yourself, you can offer suggestions, consider things as possibilities, try things on to see how they fit but never as an absolute. This is the dance you create with yourself in your life.

The reason is, shifting vibration and changing coordinates of how we live our lives, is a bit like moving house.

Even if you didn't like the old house very much and are pleased to be out of there, you still knew it very well. You knew where everything was, although you disliked it, it was comfortable and known.

Now you are in a new house, everything is in boxes; the layout of the rooms is different. You get up in the night to go to the loo to find yourself in another bedroom. You spend an hour looking in all the boxes for plates and cutlery only to give up and get a take away.

A new way can be a bit uncomfortable at first, just because you don't know it very well. But what it is, is an adventure to discover and create something new and extraordinary in life.

It would be all too easy to go back to the old house, just because you knew it really well. Take the space to get used to your new home.

THIS IS WHY MAPPING THE ENERGETIC SHIFT INTO EVERYDAY LIFE IS ESSENTIAL

Breathing Meditation

As my friend Rich says, "If I wake up breathing then I know I'm ahead."

Our breath is probably the greatest gift we have. Foremost because it keeps us alive and secondly it is our greatest tool for releasing heavy energy and finding a calm place within, a pause. We hear this in yoga, in relaxation classes, mindfulness classes, in fact almost every version of self- help work. So this is not new and yet we so easily forget we have such an incredible asset and it costs nothing, only our personal commitment.

For the purpose of our exercise I would like you to make sure that you are comfortable. If this means you sit on a chair or stand then this is fine. Or you can sit comfortably on the floor provided you can keep your back straight without any discomfort. The important thing is our posture. You want your back to be straight, your shoulders to be back and your head to be in position looking forward.

This allows us to get our breath as deeply into the belly as possible and allows the energy flow up and down the spine to move freely. If we are hunched up or bent over or uncomfortable then the energy cannot flow. And we want flow!

This meditation is not about suffering, it is about being gentle and listening to our bodies. So begin by taking a few breaths in and out through your nose, place your tongue lightly behind your top front teeth and keep your teeth just slightly apart. Relax your jaw and your face.

Now take a deep breath in through your nose, feel the air coming in, what temperature is it? Feel your abdomen expanding as the air comes in and fills your lungs. We want to take the breath as deeply within as we can. Notice at the top of your in breath there is a moment when nothing happens. A pause. Then you release the air again through your nose. Again observe how that air feels as it is released back out into the atmosphere, noticing your abdomen deflating as the air is expelled. Then again at the end of your out breath there is about a second of nothing until you breathe in again.

Repeat this slowly for a few breaths, noticing the pause at the top and bottom of each breath. This is a moment of stillness. It may be tiny but it exists. Now we want to incorporate this into our meditation.

STEP 1
Take your arms behind your back with your hands/fingers pointing down in the direction of the earth. Imagine that there is a cord of light coming from you and extending deep down into the earth, deep down into the deep dark rich soil. Keeping your spine straight and your arms extended behind you, begin breathing as above in and out through your nose.

Keep this going for a good minute or two, then take a deep breath in and release. Now take three short breaths in through your nose, imagine you are going up in a lift taking your breath higher and then hold your breath.

As you do this you want to imagine that you are pulling up energy from the earth. To do this we use our perineum muscle, this is the tiny muscle between the anus and the vagina or testicles. Hold for a count of about twelve and then release the air slowly through your nose.

Pause by gently bringing your hands to your lap and take a moment to notice how you are experiencing this, what is happening within your body, your mind?

STEP 2

Now extend your arms up above your head, your hands/fingers pointing up. It is really important to keep your body comfortable so if it hurts to fully extend your arms rest them on your head and point your hands to the sky or keep your hands in prayer position level with your chest. Imagine that incredible thread of light extending out from you into the sky to our star the sun.

Then begin your breathing in and out through your nose as you did in step one. Do this for a minute or two, take a cleansing breath, then three short breaths going up in the lift and hold for a count of twelve. Again as you pulse you are going to use the perineum and pull energy down from the universe. After a count between twelve and sixteen release the breath slowly through the nose.

Take a moment to pause and notice how you are experiencing this mixing of energy. Observe what you are experiencing.

Then you will repeat step one and step two another two times. On the third repetition, if you can, increase the speed of your breathing a little. This is called the fire breath and the speeding up of the breath increases the energy within you and this helps you to combust and eliminate toxicity on an energetic, emotional and physical level.

FOR BREATHING EXERCISE- POSITIONS

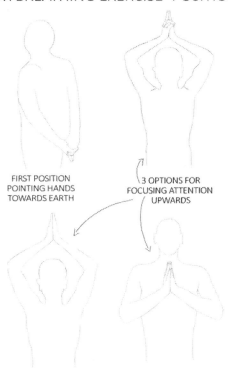

FIRST POSITION
POINTING HANDS
TOWARDS EARTH

3 OPTIONS FOR
FOCUSING ATTENTION
UPWARDS

STEP 3

Once you have completed the three rounds of breathing you come to a place of stillness. Now you reach up above your head about six inches and feel for a beautiful ball of golden light known as the wiracocha, meaning the source of the sacred. If you are not sure if you are doing this right then take a breath and imagine a luminescent globe of light above your head.

Take your hands up to this golden light and gently sense this energy, if you can sense nothing, imagine what and how you may experience this golden sphere of light. Be open to the experience.

Now taking your hands up inside this golden ball, I want you to open this energy out and bring it down and around you, taking your arms out to the side so that this energy envelops you like a soft warm blanket. This is your own personal sacred space and for the sake of detail the golden orb is your eighth chakra. So you are opening this chakra out and around you. Take a few moments to be with your experience.

This action creates a place where you can align yourself with spirit, and as you do this, your luminous energy field can expand out to the limits of your sacred space. A similar feeling may be when you have been walking in nature and you feel expansive as opposed to how you may feel in a shopping centre.

Opening your eighth chakra gives your energy body the opportunity to expand outwards and you an opportunity to get a sense of yourself. We call it a bit of self-maintenance when you can clear up or repair any holes or areas that need attention.

The true beauty of this space is that you can open this energy around you and another. A space is created where others feel safe to share what needs to be shared or said without fear of judgment and opinion. Where people can say or share things that have remained hidden for years. And even in situations on a daily basis, in moments of confrontation you can open this space silently and with your intention to help you increase your level of engagement, so that you have an opportunity to respond for the highest possible outcome. It provides a moment to centre yourself, so that you can remain still inside and so clear about what needs to be said or done, if anything. The stillness and the pause allow for more clarity about a situation and help us to stay in a place of response rather than reaction.

The breathing meditation is a commitment you make to yourself and I encourage you to make this commitment. I did every morning for over three years when I first began my training. It was a challenge, with two children under four, working etc. The mornings were hectic. What I found was that I would be in my bedroom in the middle of the meditation and one or both of my boys would come and sit next to me or on my lap.

At first I was a little put out because this was my time, but then I realized that when I was in that sacred space they were too and they loved it. What a gift.

What it showed me is that as kids we know this force is a part of our being, regardless of what we want to call it. We know it. As we grow older with the influences that we experience we forget, but it gives me confidence that we can all retrieve that knowing, that knowing that resides within each and every one of us. We have never been disconnected, we just forgot that this force is available to us always. We only talk about connection because we think we are disconnected. If we have to connect then we must be disconnected. But we have never been connected or disconnected; this source is always there.

Stillness and Meditation

It may be easy to be still and quiet our minds on a mountain or in woodlands (and this is good practice); the challenge is to bring this into every moment of everyday life. When we can do this then we are truly able to be in the flow. I wanted to say mastered the discipline but am hesitant because I know there is always more to learn. In fact the more I experience, the more I integrate, the more I realize I am forever an apprentice of life and the encounters it brings me, or should I say the encounters that I create.

So you have already the breathing meditation. There are many breath exercises found in yoga and other disciplines, like singing, for example, which train and assist us to use our breath in a positive way.

One lovely and easy exercise I learned a long time ago in my philosophy class was to focus on the senses with the breath. It takes two minutes and you can do this anywhere without causing people to raise an eyebrow or look at you as if you have landed from outer space.

Sense Awareness Exercise

(originally from a philosophy class I took many years ago)

Begin by taking a breath in – notice if you are breathing from your belly or your chest. Ideally you want to breathe as deeply as you can.

As you exhale really squeeze as much air out as possible. When we inhale and exhale from a shallow breath we leave old stale air in the base of our lungs, we want to bring in a full lung of air and expel every last bit of stale air.

This exercise in itself can rejuvenate us and increase our energy levels.

So begin with a couple of deep breaths then

a)   Focus your attention on the sense of touch, be aware of the clothes you are wearing touching your skin, the pressure of your hands on your lap, become really aware of the sense of touch.

Take a breath

b)   Then bring your awareness slowly up to your sense of taste – what tastes have you in your mouth? Is it toothpaste, garlic, lunch, coffee, what do you taste?

Take a breath

c)   Now bring your awareness to your sense of smell, what can you smell? Perfumes, flowers, exhaust fumes, food, and drink.

Take a breath

d)   Bring your awareness to your vision, what do you see, bring your full awareness to what you see around you. Then close your eyes and focus on your internal vision what do you see?

Take a breath

e)   Now bring your awareness to your sense of hearing, what do you hear? How do you hear? Is the sound loud, soft, is it near or far. Allow your hearing to run out into the distance – to the place where sound comes from and to which it returns

A place of silence, of pause and of stillness

f) Bring yourself back fully to where you are – at home, the office, the bus, train etc. etc.

This exercise can be done in a couple of minutes, it is realistic, and you can find two minutes in the day to pause.

Another simple exercise is to bring yourself fully present to your meal when you eat. Take a deep breath, pause, and appreciate for a moment the food in front of you.

As you eat really pay attention to the flavours and the experience of eating. So many of us seem to eat on the run these days, I want to emphasize that we gain more from our food if we can sit and appreciate it, even if just for a few minutes.

And chew, I remember saying to my children chew your food really well because your stomach doesn't have teeth! The more you chew your food the richer the experience. You eat slower, yes and feel full because the food has time to get to your stomach. I remember reading that it is recommended that we chew each mouthful up to thirty times. This is something that you can do every day even if it is just one meal during the day or every couple of days, you have to start somewhere.

Vision Quest

The vision quest is an ancient tool that has been used for generations by aboriginal cultures at times of change and transition. In our modern world we become so distracted by our exterior world and our thoughts that we begin to lose touch with our senses, and embarking on a vision quest is a great way to lose our mind and get back to our senses. A quest can provide us with the opportunity to take a pause in our busy lives to listen to our inner voice and to get to know ourselves on a deeper level. There are many forms of quest that you can embark upon and one of my favourite books is *Quest* by Denise Linn. I recommend that you read this if you are interested in delving further into this practice.

Here I share with you a simple version of a quest that you can create in your own garden or in the local woods if you choose. You can embark upon the quest alone or you can organize to do this with friends. It is sometimes a lovely experience to share with people you trust and love as together you can relax into the process knowing that others are there to watch over you. You can also set up simple quests for children where they get the opportunity to watch nature even if they sit still for ten to fifteen minutes.

I normally facilitate vision quests for eight hours but the length of time that you spend in your quest is entirely up to you. I would suggest a minimum of two hours. Normally the process begins as soon as you decide to embark upon a quest. It is a good idea to reduce your food intake a few days before your quest. Normally we would fast during the whole quest as this allows the preoccupation with food to be taken out of the equation. If you want to eat or for medical reasons you have to then keep the food simple like nuts and fruit and eat with conscious gratitude. Make sure you have water to drink.

How to Set Up Your Own Vision Quest

The important part of the process is to decide when and where and for how long. Then you can begin to look at what is your intention for your quest. Maybe it is to allow yourself time to pause, to take a breath, or maybe you have a question about your life and you are looking for insights. I use the following questions to help others get a sense of what they are searching for. Spend just five minutes completing this form, any longer than that and you are thinking too much.

How do you feel about the following aspects of your life on a scale of one to ten? Here, one is rubbish and ten is great.

MONEY/ PROSPERITY	LEISURE TIME	RELATIONSHIPS
FAMILY	HEALTH	CREATIVITY POTENTIAL
SPIRITUAL GROWTH	WORK/ CAREER	FRIENDS/ SUPPORT NETWORK

What activities/relationships do you want to devote more time to?

What brings you peace or joy or feels exciting?

What do you want to spend less time doing?

Who or what do you want to stop seeing/doing altogether?

What or who brings your energy down?

What are your major goals or dreams for the next twelve months?

And how will you know if you have been successful?

Once you have decided when and where, you want to know how to create a medicine wheel circle. A medicine wheel is a sacred space in nature where you may stay for anything from a few hours to four days. Traditionally you can define the space with stones or twigs. It is a good idea to make the circle large enough to lie down in but not larger than twelve feet in diameter.

Before you take the journey to find the area you will quest in it is important to stop all noise and this includes talking. Normally we do a short ceremony that takes us into silence and then the only voice that you hear after is the voice of the facilitator. If you are doing your quest alone then you can create a small ceremony to go into silence. From this moment on there is no speaking and you undertake your vision quest.

When you have chosen the area you are going to use for your quest you begin to create your sacred space by calling in stones to represent the four directions. Walk slowly, make your intention and focus on one direction at a time. I use a medicine wheel that comes from the North Native Americans. You see it is a different map but still takes you around the cardinal points and brings you to a place where you rest in the centre of yourself.

MEDICINE WHEEL FOR VISION QUEST
NORTH NATIVE AMERICAN

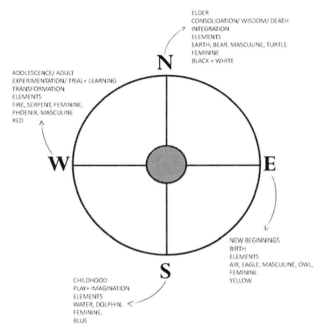

ELDER
CONSOLIDATION/ WISDOM/ DEATH
INTEGRATION
ELEMENTS
EARTH, BEAR, MASCULINE, TURTLE
FEMININE
BLACK + WHITE

N

ADOLESCENCE/ ADULT
EXPERIMENTATION/ TRIAL+ LEARNING
TRANSFORMATION
ELEMENTS
FIRE, SERPENT, FEMININE,
PHOENIX, MASCULINE
RED

W

E

S

NEW BEGINNINGS
BIRTH
ELEMENTS
AIR, EAGLE, MASCULINE, OWL,
FEMININE.
YELLOW

CHILDHOOD
PLAY+ IMAGINATION
ELEMENTS
WATER, DOLPHIN,
FEMININE.
BLUE

So there are many maps and this particular medicine wheel begins in the East, which represents new beginnings like the morning sun rising over the horizon, the dawn of a new day. This is the place of birth, of the element air and the power animals of Eagle representing the masculine and Owl representing the feminine and the colour yellow like the sun.

Then in the South we find the place of childhood, of play, of imagination, of emotions of nurturing, represented by the element water and the power animals, dolphin representing the feminine and frog representing the masculine and the colour blue as of water.

In the West we find the place of adolescence and adulthood, the place of ideas, of experimentation, trial and error transformation, represented by the element of fire and the power animal Phoenix representing the masculine and Serpent representing the feminine and the colour red as of fire.

In the North we find the place of the elder, grandfather, grandmother, the place of integration, consolidation of wisdom, represented by the element of earth and the power animal Bear representing the masculine and Turtle representing the feminine and the colour black and white.

Once you have your four directions in place you can fill in between with sticks so what you create is a circle. Then when complete walk around the outside of your circle clockwise three times and then enter by the East. As you enter, make a circle with your hand and say, "To all my relations" or "A ho matak weahsun" (phonetic Cherokee). This is a reminder that whatever healing work we do on ourselves benefits all and that we can call on the power of the ancestors to assist us in our quest. Then you offer gifts to the four directions, the Mother Earth and to Great Spirit. Traditionally these are cornmeal, tobacco or other herbs. You can however use whatever you feel or sense is appropriate. You can use salt to absorb and transform negativity and you can sprinkle this around the edge of the circle.

If during your quest you need to leave your circle to go to the toilet or for any reason you leave from the East and as you exit the East direction you again say, "To all my relations"; this is repeated each time you exit and enter your circle.

You see how each map is slightly different but follows the cycles of our life's journey as we grow and is also representative of areas of our lives that come up looking for attention as we make our epic journey. It is another map but one that supports our growth and empowers us to learn and move on in our lives. Many great things have come from vision quests where again you can take the opportunity to raise your own energetic vibration and we use this as a tool to bring us to a moment of quiet and stillness so we cannot ignore or pretend that we have not seen something about ourselves.

In Grandfather's teachings he describes all these maps as tools to get us back to a place where we can know ourselves and communicate with the natural world, where our relationship is truly participatory and we are fully aware of our impact and the consequences of our beliefs, feelings and behaviours on the world around us. He says that our ancestors had direct access to this but created tools that we could use as a crutch as he calls it to get us back to a relationship in the world that was once natural to us.

Normally I would use a drum to send people out to their quest and to bring them back. However you can ask your friends to call you back in whatever way you wish or if you are alone you may have your watch in your bag that you can refer to as long as you keep its location a secret from yourself for the majority of the time you are questing. Or you can surrender to the experience and return when you sense you are ready. Be careful here though because sitting with ourselves in nature is not something we do often so watch out for the feelings of boredom or frustration that may cause you to step out of your quest too early. The point of the quest is to ride these waves until we come to the quiet place within. Then we can begin to see and sense answers or insights that we would otherwise miss.

People often ask, what shall I do in my circle? If you have to do anything you can keep a journal close so that you can write during your experience or you can create what we call a prayer stick. The prayer stick has been used by native people for thousands of years in many different parts of the world. It is made by winding wool, leather and twine around a stick and attaching other natural objects to it. At least one feather was always added as a symbol of the Great Spirit.

You can use the prayer stick as a bridge between the world of spirit and matter to manifest your dreams. You can create a prayer stick to release outmoded ways of being. You can weave all you want to move away from on to the stick then either burn it or float it down a fast moving river. You can use the prayer stick to weave in all that you are grateful for in your life. Again what you choose to do with the stick afterwards is up to you. You can keep it as a symbol of your quest or you can give it to fire, bury it in the earth or give it to a body of fast moving water.

In the Cherokee tradition the prayer stick is placed where the first rays of the rising sun will fall upon it and then either left there or taken into the weaver's dwelling place as a reminder of the intention of the prayers. Some tribes leave the prayer stick upright in the earth. Your prayer stick is a unique expression of you.

As you return from your quest the silence remains until a short ceremony to bring you from the silence into a circle, where you have the opportunity to share your experience. This is done using the talking stick. Placed in the centre of the circle the talking stick is used to acknowledge everyone present and only the person with the talking stick speaks. The very first words spoken after a vision quest are often very powerful and I have seen people, even after a quest of two hours, finding it hard to break the silence. If you are on your own you may want to journal or read out from your journal so you hear your voice. Or you may choose to share with another person close to you. The power is often in the sharing as it brings the experience from the mythic realm into the everyday.

Once the sharing is complete there can be a meal to celebrate and this can be followed by the creation of a treasure map. I explained how to create this earlier. Take a piece of paper create a circle the size of a dinner plate or medium round tray. Then take a handful of magazines and take thirty minutes to flick through them, taking out any images or words that catch your attention. Then glue these on to your circle. After thirty minutes stop, step back and take a look at what you have created and then share the meaning of the images and words. Once everyone has a sense of the energy of your treasure map you can hold the energy and surrounding it in a bubble allow it to float out into the universe, where those dreams can manifest in ways you would perhaps never consider if you were to think about them.

If all this sounds a little too complicated you can simply create a sit spot where you can go on a regular basis to be quiet and with yourself for a few minutes each day or longer if you choose to. I remember creating a moment with my kids when they were younger, creating mini circles where they sat and watched the earth around them. They were amazed at the life that was going on in that small circle of space and so was I. Any space you can create where you spend a few moments in the natural world will be of the greatest service to you.

And finally:

From the moment we are born we are wired to survive. And under all the maps we create to navigate our life is a deep yearning. This is that sound of the core life force manifesting itself as you, as me. It is always there. We bury it deep with all of our distractions but it never goes away. Always present it is our essential I, the wholeness of our being, not our little identity I or ego. The journey is bringing our core self and our identity together, to a place of harmony. This essential I is a force that manifests itself in everyone and in everything, with an aim to experience the fullness of being alive, the journey towards balance. Here a light so bright shines, never to be extinguished, and it is within each one of us.

Living is all about the willingness to dance with the journey of our life. Listen to what truly makes your heart sing. Imagine what it might be if you feel you have no idea. Feel it, create an action, a tiny action every day to remind you of this life force. Remember small can be very significant.

Here are some words that came to me during a quest I was facilitating.

Once when weary and feeling lonely I stopped on a dusty track
I saw a glistening light from the corner of my eye
The road ahead looked barren, what good could possibly come
This journey really having made me so numb
Stopped in my tracks, I sat on the earth, this glistening light still catching my eye
Not forward or backward just here where I sit. I surrender in the dust
The wind blows strong, the dust engulfs me
I see nothing, I am still I do not move
The rain comes and washes away the dust, I am still and I do not move
The sun comes and dries everything bringing light and warmth, I am still and I do not move
The night brings moon and stars and darkness, I am still and I do not move
The day brings light, sun and colour, I am still and I do not move

*Everything is moving, shifting, changing and yet the glistening
light remains here I can see it, feel it, taste it, smell it, touch it
even hear it*
This tiny light glistens and shines – for me
A tiny light and it is tiny and it is me
*My heart singing I remain sitting with this tiny light shining and
glistening*
*This is mine, it is all that I have, but it is mine and with gratitude
I sit on the earth in the centre of the dusty track*
This light so tiny is so bright and cannot be extinguished
Moving or still, sun or rain, light or dark, hot or cold
It is always here, never to be extinguished
This tiny light of mine.

Chapter 4

The Insights of the Journey Around the Shamanic Medicine Wheel

The Medicine Wheel

As quoted in the Tao
The great Tao
Has no expectations for me,
No demands, no battles
Or wars to fight
And no history
To live up to

The shamanic path follows the same rhythm as the compass and depending on which set of teachings you follow you begin your journey in a particular direction. I am sharing my experience of the shamanic path of the Q'ero shaman and so for the purpose of this book we begin in the South. The South is the beginning point anchored by the southern star, which is the only star in our universe that does not move. So we follow a circular path, which is known as the medicine wheel, and we pass through the South, West, North and East. Each direction contains within it a set of experiential teachings that in themselves are not magic but when applied to our lives enable us to create and experience magic and life turns from ordinary into extraordinary.

South and West directions

Our Story and Why We Never See Our Treasure

It's funny sitting here, I'm with some very good friends of mine and whilst I am outside enjoying the October sunshine they are in the process of clearing out the loft in one of their barns.

A suitcase has just come down that looks like it could have been stashed away for ten years or more, full of clothes and bits and bobs – old memories, old shoes once loved but know knackered and well beyond repair, clothes that no longer fit. Boxes and bags full of lifetimes passed, of memories and a lot of goodness knows what!

And as all this stuff is pulled out, underneath sits a beautiful old table and some really old photos. Real treasures. The sad thing is you don't see the treasures or even use them because they're covered over by a load of stuff. A load of stuff that right now is no longer of service. And this is a bit how we live our lives.

Our Story

We find ourselves in a life that at this point is the current episode in a long story reaching far back to our birth. Well that's the start as far as we are aware right now. This story is full of its experiences, influences, and beliefs and has created a map. An incredible map that holds us in this life we find ourselves in. All those coordinates that created the path we have taken, the decisions and choices we have made and continue to make.

Maybe you like your life, maybe life is hard or maybe an area of your life is not going so great or an area of your life is fantastic in relation to the rest.

The bottom line is, it is all part of a story that we tell about ourselves that supports the identity that we have created for the world to see.

You will remember, I hope, that I suggested that life is based on perception and that perception is a learned phenomenon. Taking this into consideration, the identity you have created, the map you have created for life, is based, perhaps, on many influences external to you, influences that determined how you created the coordinates to survive life. We are wired to survive, from the moment we are born, so it goes without saying that depending on our personal experiences and external influences we will create a map, an identity and story to get us through. A strategy if you like to survive life, the life we have known.

Basically everything we learn comes from past beliefs and influences that come from much further back in time. Let alone the influence of our society, our culture and religious beliefs. So you know that old cliché 'well you chose this life, you always have a choice'.

Yes of course we have a choice and we did choose and continue to do so. The choices are based on what? Our true self? Or the self that has been created by external influences? Which belief? Which thought? Which actions? Which habits? Which values? Where did it come from? Is it all ours?

It is essential, yes, that we are guided as children by those around us so that we can function in the family, society, culture that we have been born into. On the other hand we can lose contact with who we truly are. It becomes more and more tricky to establish our truth when this treasure is buried under so much other stuff.

We all have a story of our life and this story continues, of course it does, being a shaman does not mean that life becomes a bed of rose petals believe me. What we experience in our lives can be down to simply how much of the old story we insist on carrying around with us. You know like all those old suitcases up in the loft or down in the cellar. Full of old memories and clothes that are out dated and no longer of service but we still want to hang onto them. How heavy is this? How much energy does it take to keep everything in boxes and suitcases and then carry them everywhere?

Then one day we wake up and we realize that it is simply a story. It is a story that we tell but it is not who we truly are. Yes, the experiences have moulded us into the person and character we are, whether others deem this good or bad.

To recognize this can be a scary place because our identity is based on this story, the way that we present ourselves to the world is based on this story. If we clear out the loft and the cellar, what will be left?

Not much you may think, but just stop for one moment and recall the treasures under the suitcases hidden from sight. This is what is available to us when we have the courage to honour our story for what it is. The treasures in our story are what we want to move on with in our lives. These treasures may be the things we have learned about ourselves and the wisdom gained from the experiences we have had. Our journey involves honouring our story, giving thanks and taking a moment to reflect and to find the nugget of gold, the wisdom gained, even in the most hideous of places. It is a place where we have the opportunity to move on in life with a few treasures instead of having to carry all those bags and suitcases around with us. By coming to a place of reconciliation we can heal our wounds and move on. We can stop reliving the old hurts and mistakes. We can stop using the world around us in an effort to heal our hurt. We can take the wisdom we have gained and use this in service of others. We can turn our anger, our jealousy, our unworthiness, our sadness and our trauma into places of power, compassion and understanding.

Now I am not about to suggest that this is easy, far from it. I know only too well how deep I have had to go to find treasures. I will mention here my understanding of forgiveness. Forgiveness is not about condoning someone's behaviour; it is about giving up the hope that yesterday could have been better. It wasn't and it never will be. It is done, it is in the past and nothing we do or say will change the event or the circumstances. What we do have is the opportunity to see what it taught us personally and if the answer is for the moment nothing, then honour nothing. It has to be better than carrying that heavy stuff around.

We all love a good story; we all add words here and there or take words out to make it either more interesting, create more of a drama or leave stuff out in order that something is not seen or told, something we want to hide about ourselves. It is human nature to like a good story, to add a bit of drama and shows great creative skill, something I sense we all have. The trouble is we start to believe the story and forget what really happened. And so it is with the story of our life. We believe we are the story. We forget who we truly are, that we have the potential to be so much more than the story we tell. It is a story. Perhaps an exciting, tragic, happy, sad, incredible story and yet it is a story.

We create stories all the time; if not outwardly our interior voice is constantly giving us a running commentary of the day. A little trick we have learned at home is to use the full stop. When something happens and you know that it looks like the drama is going to kick off one of us will say, "OK what happened?" And after the response we say, "OK, put a full stop on the end of that sentence." Now we know that the rest is the story and what we are making the event mean about ourselves, and those around us. It has really helped in some situations that I know would have got really heated and it has given everyone a chance to take a breath and reflect for a moment. It is a matter of staying awake and shifting the level at which we engage with each other or the world around us. Can't say that it has always stopped the drama but it has helped on many occasions to keep things clean and much easier to deal with.

So the FULL STOP does work. Try it, just try it and see. You may find your internal voice will continue to ramble on. Be awake enough to ask yourself why. What part of this drama is showing you something about yourself?

The shamanic teachings tell us that if we can honestly and without any self-deception confront our life story and the reason why we hang on to it, we can begin to use it as an opportunity to honour the circumstances and the people involved. We can quietly contemplate the gift or learning for us. In honouring we allow ourselves to move on in life, taking the wisdom from the experience with us. Let us be realistic here; if we do not get the learning the lesson will just keep on occurring until we do and this is how patterns become so embedded, not just in our individual life circumstances but in family lines, cultures, society and in faith and religion.

When we can take the old stories and patterns and treat them like dear old friends, loyal and honourable old friends, we are acknowledging that somewhere, sometime they have served us or someone well, because somewhere we hold that this is true. However, there can be many times when these patterns stop us from being fully available for our life right now, they stop us from making a decision based on what is here in the moment, instead creating a repeat performance by taking everything we have known and throwing it out in front of us to live back into.

So just like an old friend we want to honour these times in our lives, accept the learning or the gift and this means we can begin to move on in life. Now it does not mean that the events never took place. Yes they did and by honouring them you no longer have to carry the story with you everywhere you go. They remain a part of your life experience but now you realize they are not who you are. We can never underestimate the power of honouring. This is not some worshipping act but an acknowledgement of what happened and a choice to move on in life with the treasure, the learning and insight we have become aware of.

Within our stories are the many roles we play. So as the director and producer of our life story we also create many roles. The interesting thing with roles is that they are something that we can end up possessing and in turn they begin to possess us. With any role, whether this is the role of mother, father, CEO, teenager to name a few, each comes with a set of our own expectations of us in this role and our perception of what we think others expect of us in this role. In fact the role can become so defined that there is no room for movement and we miss opportunities within the role we are playing purely because we become bound by our beliefs and expectations of these roles. It is a useful guide to look at what role we feel we are playing in any given situation and then look at unbinding ourselves from our own limitations within this role. You see the shaman knows that every role we play has its own destiny line and so often if we get fixated on a certain role or define ourselves by this role then we find ourselves heading in one direction only, believing we have no option but to continue the way we always have.

The shaman recognizes that we want to unbind ourselves from all the roles that we play. By doing this it does not mean that we no longer play these parts in our lives. What it means is, that we have much more energy available to step into these roles from a new place, open to more opportunities than we could ever imagine. If you can imagine; you begin to sit at the centre of your life and recognize as you step into each role, bringing yourself fully to the moment, adding value and purpose to the role you are playing and you begin to experience life very differently. All these aspects show up in your story. Sometimes it is a useful exercise when situations arise to ask yourself, what role am I playing here? You may find you are playing the victim role, or the stupid role, or the role of Mum or Dad or nurse or doctor. Take a moment to look at how you define yourself within this role based on your expectations and the perceived expectations of others. You will have the opportunity to use the nature painting and other shamanic methods to unbind yourself from limiting scripts. The beauty of the shamanic way is that there is no need to get caught up in the detail. The less detail the better and the more opportunity there is for a shift. I remember the very first time I did this, the first time I brought into my awareness all the roles I played in my life.

I started with mother, then I added wife, then I added shaman and by that time I felt suffocated, physically I could not get a deep breath. I was astounded. At this time in my life, I had identified myself so strongly with just these three roles that they had taken over my whole life. I had no idea that I had placed so much meaning onto these roles. Bringing this into my awareness also showed up lots of emotional feelings, Love, excitement, dedication, anger, resentment and exhaustion, to name a few.

A whole lot of stuff popped up before I could go any further with my list and I had a long list of roles. Just like our stories, we begin to believe the roles that we play are actually who we are. Doing this exercise revealed to me that I identified myself so strongly with these three roles at this time and that I was so consumed by them that I had little energy for any of them let alone any other role I may have been playing at the time.

We are all so much more than the roles we play. By becoming consumed by them we have no energy available for living, for creating and participating in anything else other than the roles we identify ourselves with. Our roles, like our stories, define who we are and keep us tightly held in a certain way of being, certain beliefs, behaviours, with very little if no room or energy to even begin considering something different. Why; because each one of these roles has a destiny line that comes from the past and reaches out into the future. It holds a particular path with a particular momentum going in a certain direction.

By consciously naming all our roles, it gives us the opportunity to stay in the centre of ourselves and to be aware and awake as we step into each role rather than being driven in a certain direction because we believe this is who we are and all we ever can be.

Do you see the difference?

I am at the centre of my being aware of all the roles that I play. Then I choose how and when I step into those roles. I am piloting my life because I am aware that this is purely a role I am playing in this moment and perhaps in two hours' time I will step into another role. Each time though I come back to my centre to remember who I am. I am directing this play. If I become consumed by the roles something other than my true self is directing my life. I may be comfortable and be able to take a snooze, but is this role taking me in the direction I really want to go?

Legend and law says that destiny is available to anyone in any moment. Fate is something that is decided based on the past and the current momentum.

The difference is about the value and purpose you bring to your life and you have to show up for it. We can bring value and purpose to the simplest of tasks and experience a life full of meaning and we can also be the director or in charge of a team and our life can be missing the value, purpose and meaning we are searching for. Sometimes it can be a simple task of unbinding ourselves from old outmoded beliefs and strategies for the role that we are playing and we suddenly find the value and meaning, realizing it was always there; we just didn't see it.

Your Story

So now it's your turn, take ten minutes and write your story. Take a look at the story you present to the world of who you are and where you have come from.

Take a moment to sit quietly with this story, acknowledging every aspect of its content. If there was one thing, one thing your story teaches you, what is it? What might it be? If it is not obvious, and it rarely is, imagine what it might be. Here you are engaging with your story from the level of the physical and emotional or Serpent and Jaguar. Be aware of the leading role you are playing and take a look at how you define yourself by this role. There may be more than one role; make a note in your journal so you have something to refer to when you come to create your nature painting.

Now if this seems a little mundane or too much writing, imagine your life as a river, let's take it to the world of imagery and use the level of engagement at the mythic. Hummingbird. You can begin once upon a time there was a river and then let the story unfold.

How does your river flow?
Where does you river flow?
Does your river flow or is it damned up?
Are there waterfalls, underground caverns?
Where is the source of your river?
Are there any obstacles?
Maybe there have been and you have found your way around them?
Is there debris in the water?
Is it shallow, deep, both?
Warm, cold?
Fast moving, slow?

Get the sense of your life as a river, allowing it to reveal itself. Again take some time to reflect on what shows up. When we use imagery we can go to the source of the issue so rather than keep moving stuff around, we can make a small adjustment at the source of our river and the whole river will respond. This is where we reconcile those memories in our energy field, the original memory or wound, and then we shift our energetic vibration. Then we can be available for a different experience to the one we know so well.

The easiest way to shift anything is when it is not solid. So a shaman tool is to release heavy energy (in the form of emotions, beliefs, thoughts etc.) in the realm of the energetic where you are dealing with ninety-nine percent energy and one percent matter. This is far easier than trying to move a whole house. So here is an opportunity to use the nature painting described at the beginning of the book. As you reflect on your story, whichever way you have looked at it, you are looking to get a sense of a core theme that shows itself. If you are unable to get the sense of a core theme close your eyes and feel what is going on inside of you. Because sometimes we are unaware of the origin of issues we are facing in our life, using the feelings in our body is the best way to begin because our body does not lie. Our mind on the other hand will make up all sorts of reasons why and why not. So just go with your feelings if you are not sure where to start.

As you reflect, call in the organizing principles of the universe. You can use the prayer at the beginning of this book or create your own. Remember it is your intention and the feeling in your heart that brings you into alignment with these forces of creation. Create your circle and choose an item to represent you. Blow your energy into this and place it in the centre of your circle. Then as you reflect on your story observe your energy in the way of emotions, thoughts etc.; the easiest way to begin to shift this is by taking small objects from nature and blow all the stuff out of your body into the natural items. This can be sticks, flowers and stones. Then you can leave them outside in your nature painting to work with nature, which uses that heavy energy as manure to help the trees and the plants grow. In nature, in the realm of energy, there is no judgment, just the force of alchemy where heavy energy can be transformed into manure to grow and nourish life. You are beginning to take charge of your inner garden.

If you are thinking, how on earth can this help?

Great, I did the same and believe me it does.

The shifts can be so subtle that you may not even realize and they may not be immediate. But what I will say is that as you release heavy suitcases of stuff, your energetic vibration will shift and things will begin to reorganize themselves internally and externally around you.

You will find yourself in a situation one day, walk away and say, "That was different." How do I know? Because I have experienced it.

Now if you hold a belief that nothing ever works, then I can guarantee that you will perceive that it does not work. As a shaman we know that any belief is self-fulfilling and we would ask you to consider the payoff or the benefit you may have for this belief. You have to be prepared to have the experience and I encourage you to do so. We are complex, we humans, that is for sure and that is why there is no fast answer. Only an adventure and a tough one because we have to wake up and stay awake to the paradigm that we model our lives upon. The word paradigm means a typical example or pattern or model and paradigms power our perception and our perceptions power our emotions. Most of our emotional responses are to our perceptions, which remember are a learned phenomena or what you think is true about a given situation. Remember if your perception is false then your emotional response to it will be false too. Check your perceptions and beyond that check the truth of your model or paradigm and what you believe. Just because you believe something firmly does not make it true. Be willing to re-examine what you believe.

By taking your story of your life into the mythic it provides you with an opportunity to look at your story from a different place, it provides a place where you may begin to see the treasures and most importantly recognize that this is the story you tell but it is not who you are. You have the potential to be so much more than the story you once told. As soon as you begin this process you are saying to the universe I am willing to step away from this old story and begin taking the treasures of my experiences and moving forward in my life.

Chapter 5

The Beliefs, Patterns and Shadows Bound in Our Story

We all have beliefs which, along with a whole mix of other things, are perceptions about life that we have learned and decided upon as true for us. They are also fundamental in the foundations of the identity and world we create around ourselves and they are themselves self-fulfilling prophecies. There are always red flags that highlight beliefs and patterns but in amongst everyday life they get lost and are easily ignored or even if we see them we choose not to shift because we consider that the payoff for this pattern or belief is deemed too great a prize. Absurd as this may look from an outsider's point of view the things that we hang on to, we do for a reason. Most of the time it gives us the exact opposite of what we believe its purpose is but for some reason or strategy, whether we are aware of it or not, it exists within us and runs our life.

So in our stories we find a mix of the above and in order to recognize what it is that is showing up in the script of the story we tell we have to have an understanding of the way in which these elements work so that we can recognize them.

Patterns can show up in any area of our life and are normally driven by a core belief. They can come from a source much deeper than we can see. The challenge with patterns is that they are very well hidden and operate often under cover with the prime reason that you will not be able to see them. The energy contained in these patterns is very strong and the pattern itself demands that the people involved will behave in a certain way, a way which reinforces the pattern and reaffirms its very survival.

Remember somewhere we believe or consider that these patterns serve us. A pattern is driven by a past experience and everything that someone, maybe us, made it mean. Any pattern is consuming energy and taking up valuable space in our luminous energy field, affecting our energy, stopping us from being available for our life.

It is a bit like having too many icons on your computer screen and so many programs running that the computer becomes very slow to respond to new demands. This is how our luminous body gets and how once this becomes overloaded our physical body and our lives are affected. Our energy becomes slow and dense, we become heavier and heavier carrying these programs around until there is nothing left to experience life in the moment. It is self-fulfilling in that because there is no energy available, (computer memory space), we just keep throwing the past out into the future, creating more of the same purely because we do not have the energy to live into something completely new. It seems easier to just live in the past even though we are drained, tired and fed up with having the same kind of experiences.

So here sit our stories and in our stories are our experiences, our beliefs and our patterns. Some of these are ours and some are those of our family, the society and culture that we have been born into. Consider that with any pattern you become like a magnet and you attract similar things back into your life and this continues until you discover the pattern and to do this you have to be awake and aware. Once you discover a pattern you are almost there. By naming the pattern you can begin to honour the origins, acknowledge the reasons why and begin to establish the learning. This then enables you to create a new coordinate for your map of your life taking the treasure only. Just like periodically clearing out your computer of old programs that are out of date and freeing up space for the new updated programs that you could really use right now.

Patterns can be tricky to shift by ourselves because we are not always the best at being objective and also because our identity is very clever at fooling us into thinking that we have dealt with it, the pattern that is. Why? Because our identity is dependent upon this pattern so this part of us is not too happy about letting the pattern go. The reason is simply because the pattern is all we have ever known and we deem it essential to our survival even though it may be hurting us or those around us.

Generations and Karma

Each one of us is a daughter or a son to a Mum and Dad who themselves were sons and daughters. Every one of us carries some patterns or beliefs from the past simply because this is how we learn about life when we are young.

As we observe those around us both in words and actions, we make decisions about our lives. We create strategies, beliefs, and behaviours and sometimes there are those patterns that are passed on but we are not even consciously aware of them. They are simply part of a pattern that continues to repeat itself generation after generation.

Not all patterns are good or bad, I know, I know. I thought the same. There are some characteristics I have inherited from my parents that I like. Great, as long as I realize and know them, and recognize the times when they are not useful. It is important to remember that any pattern comes from the past and whilst it was useful perhaps forty years ago it may not be now.

In shaman terms it benefits us to be absolutely aware of our inherited patterns and to honour them and die to them. We can still keep humour but experience it differently. We can still keep stubborn but know what stubborn looks like for us and how and when that might be useful now rather than stubborn behaviour appearing at inappropriate moments just because that is how it has always shown up. We are not going to forget everything, please do not worry about that. The bottom line is we never will because this is a part of who we have become. In honouring the lives of our ancestors and the patterns we can begin to let go of the stories and what we have made them mean about them and us.

This is not about worship; it is about acknowledging that our ancestors, like us, were attempting to reconcile the duality that they found themselves living in.

I realized, when my mum died, that none of us really know our parents or anyone for that matter. We think we do but truly we only know them in the role that they play for us. Even if you are really close there are things that you may never know. We have no idea how another person's life has truly been, what the internal challenges have been, let alone the external ones, the decisions, the mistakes. Yes some of them perhaps, but does anyone truly know you on the inside?

I spent some time with my parents when my mum was dying and we talked about many things. This is part of the normal process and if you have the chance to be present, it is a recapitulation of someone's life (I will talk more of this later in the book). I was a witness to some insights into both of the lives of my mum and my dad that I had never known. I had no idea of some of the stories of their lives and now I have I am deeply grateful to have been given the opportunity to discover them both as people, as souls on a journey. So much of what I had judged and misunderstood came to a place of understanding. I was able to see where certain patterns and beliefs continued to inform me. They were not my beliefs or the beliefs of my parents. Interestingly they had come from much further back and I may never have known.

Here's a diagram to help show this.

Ancestor/ Genetic+ Karmic—Visuals

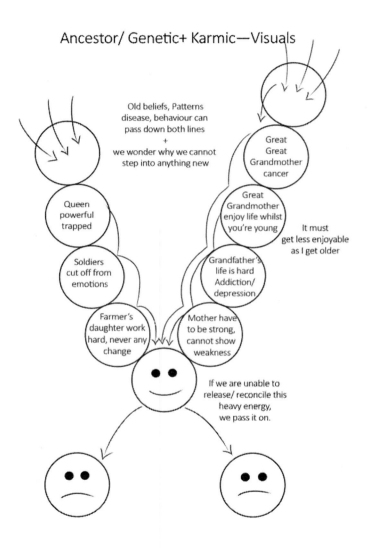

Old beliefs, Patterns disease, behaviour can pass down both lines
+
we wonder why we cannot step into anything new

Great Great Grandmother cancer

Queen powerful trapped

Great Grandmother enjoy life whilst you're young

It must get less enjoyable as I get older

Soldiers cut off from emotions

Grandfather's life is hard Addiction/ depression

Farmer's daughter work hard, never any change

Mother have to be strong, cannot show weakness

If we are unable to release/ reconcile this heavy energy, we pass it on.

The past – the generational line is taking a look at my direct ancestors. The karmic line is giving us a look at some of the stories that live within us. Karmic if you believe in past lives or if it is easier those parts that continue to live through us based on the saying 'as you sow, so shall you reap' or 'what you give out you get back at some point'. Any relationship or unfinished business has to be reconciled somewhere on our journey. Now bearing in mind we are all descendants of someone who survived a time in human evolution – it is possible we'll have a few stories informing us – even if we are not consciously aware of them.

So let's say in the generic line sits a belief or value that we have to be strong, what might you believe? That you cannot show weakness? Perhaps?

If life is hard and a struggle and drink makes it easier and beating someone gives you a sense of power you are lacking because you see yourself failing and being weak. You may believe this is the only way to feel powerful and in charge? Perhaps?

If you experienced this kind of abuse as a child you may decide you are never going to be this way. So perhaps you become passive and stubborn to ensure that you do not abuse anyone. However maybe this goes on internally and you end up with depression.

If you have to enjoy life while you're young – maybe you might believe that life gets tougher and less fun as you get older. Illnesses and physical, generic patterns can also play out down the family line.

Then we add this to the karmic stories.

If you wish for more but all you're faced with is a poor peasant's life and no matter how hard you work it is just more of the same and you are not satisfied with this.

You may believe why bother making an effort, it makes no difference anyway.

A soldier faced with violence, blood, loss and disappointment may wonder what life is all about or become strong but cut off from his emotions.

The Queen may have lived a privileged life in relation to external riches but was she starved of living as she wanted, as she was a possession of the people.

Maybe she believes it is better to have nothing and to be free than to have everything and be owned by someone.

And all of this energy, if un-reconciled, is passed down and sits in our energy field waiting for the opportunity to arise when it can finally be laid to rest. Where the wounds of the past can be healed and no longer passed down to another generation in the hope that reconciliation will happen.

Now if we take aspects of all of these – little bits of stories, beliefs, behaviours – the energy in these still runs. It is like a thin cord that attaches to us as we are born and we don't even know that we don't know. But is makes sense doesn't it? We all have many ancestors who have had to face many things so it goes without saying that those experiences and all that they created can still flow through us.

Unbinding ourselves from our Karmic and ancestral lineage

So as depicted earlier in the book now is the opportunity for you to participate in completing a diagram as I did just to get a sense of the patterns that may flow down through either your family line or let's say story (karmic) line.

At the level of the physical or Serpent you can take a sheet of paper and write down the names of ancestors that you know of or get a sense of and maybe as you do, you will also get a sense of them, of what may have been passed down the family line that you have inherited.

It is a fascinating experience. I acknowledge it is not always the easiest place to say thank you especially when our experiences have been brutal or tragic. Within all of this it does give us an opportunity to step away from the energetic binding that continues to hold us back from living our lives and of course continues through us to our children.

Remember it is not about condoning the way people have behaved and what they may have done. The experiences are there, just like our stories. Here is an opportunity to lighten our load by unbinding ourselves from the past so we can perhaps create something different, not just for us but also for our kids.

You can then take this to a nature painting, working at the level of the mythic or Hummingbird. You release emotions and feelings energetically by blowing into natural objects as you reflect on your ancestors or your karmic stories. Place these objects in the circle, a space where you can release the energy that binds you.

This is a powerful exercise as energy buried deeply has an opportunity to be released and brought into our conscious awareness. Remember awareness is the key. When we have seen, when that ray of light has shone on to something that sits in the shadows we have an opportunity to transcend it.

Once you feel that you have completed the work with your nature painting, the items can either be burned, buried or offered to your altar. You can create an altar where you can celebrate your ancestors, say thank you, maybe even find that place of forgiveness. Remember, and I have said this before, forgiveness is giving up the hope that yesterday might have been better. It in no way condones behaviour, but frees us up from attempting to change something that is done. It allows us, if we can find it in ourselves, to let go of what we cannot change in order that we can use this energy to create something more positive and fulfilling for our own lifetime and future generations. Now this is a legacy of service. By creating an altar to both our karmic and generational lines we can honour and say thank you. As we do we can begin to unravel the energy from the stories that bind us.

In earth cultures still today they have elaborate celebrations to honour their ancestors. This is not worship. It is an opportunity to say thank you and to ensure that they know where the ancestors are. On the altar and not living through them.

An altar can be however you want it to be, you can use pictures, flowers, sweets, wine, natural objects, one or more candles. You can sing, you can dance, sit quietly, and play music. It is a reflection of your own celebration of their lives. Great or small it is your intention that matters. Remember this is not about worshipping or condoning the actions of our ancestors or stories that live within us (karma – past lives).

It is about honouring the lives of people who maybe we have never known, honouring their journey, of which we know very little. It is a place of recognition that like us they were born into families, societies, cultures where evolution played a part in the circumstances they found themselves in and they did the best they could, given what they knew and remembered. Knowing that our ancestors and our stories remain in the place of the altar and the nature painting, the energy of these does not continue to live through us. We know where they are. So this is about setting up a ceremony where you can honour your ancestors and create a place for them that is not you.

Here is a beautiful and simple example of how this pattern thing works.

During a class I was teaching, the subject of patterns and shadows came up. It usually does.

I was explaining how sometimes we behave in certain ways following patterns that we are not even remotely aware of and a participant asked if he could share what he recognized as a great example of this.

Every Christmas my mum buys a huge ham joint, she cuts it in two, puts it into two different trays and cooks it.

One Christmas, I asked her why she always cut the ham in two. She replied that she didn't know why exactly but it was something her mother had always done.

So I asked my Nan, "Nan, why does Mum cut the ham in two every Christmas?"

Nan replied, "I don't know why your mother does it, but I used to because I never had a tin large enough to take the large joint."

His Mum had a tin large enough but she was carrying on a behaviour and she had no idea why. Interesting isn't it?

This is a beautiful simple example that for me really illustrates how we continue to behave in ways, running beliefs and patterns from the past that we are often not aware of and can often give no explanation of.

Shadow

Within our stories and our patterns we find parts of ourselves we will not or do not want to acknowledge, known as our shadow selves. An awareness of this is essential to the shaman and can help us wake up in our daily lives.

Shadow has been and still is a large part of our human evolution. It was Carl Jung who first used the term shadow, explaining that this represented the parts of ourselves that we do not acknowledge or the parts that we want to hide from the world. He explains that the shadow is more valuable to us than our ego self, as our shadow is far closer to the truth of who we are than the ego identity we have created for the world to see. And within our patterns and our stories sit our shadows. Another way of describing shadow is all the human characteristics that we have decided do not work, or that if seen may put us in danger. So we take a decision to hide them from the world. The darkness hides the true size of our fears, lies and regrets. The truth is that they are more shadow than reality and seem bigger in the dark. The moment we bring awareness to them, shine a light into the places where they live inside of us we begin to be able to see them for what they truly are. On the other hand we may believe it is safer to keep this energy inside of us and sometimes when we are kids or even adults doing our best to survive, it really is safer. Then life changes, we have grown from the child into an adult or an adult whose circumstances have changed but unless the wounding is reconciled on the inside we are still the kid or young adult living in a dark cave surrounded by monsters and out of habit we keep adding to our collection. For we collect things we value. This is another way in which imprints and patterns are written into our energy fields and then we just keep living into them. This script that we have written is very strong and those around us can often do nothing but collude with the pattern in play. The memory that is now playing on the screen. High intense circumstances, fuelled with great emotion and actions create the icon in the memory banks only to be replayed over and over again. That is until we become aware and awake enough to honour ourselves in a different and more positive way.

Duality

We live in a world of duality
We know light only because we know dark
We know good only because we know bad
We know happy only because we know sad
We know strength because we know weakness

We live in a world of opposites and we strive, believe it or not, in our everyday lives to strike a balance between the two. It's all about creating a relationship within that holds the balance of all the opposites and we have to know ourselves really well in order to accomplish this in every moment. It is a bit like standing in the middle of a see-saw with one set of opposites on one end and the other at the other end and doing your best to maintain balance as it moves naturally up and down.

When a shaman talks about right relationship, the sense is that at all times we are in alignment within and when I say this I mean that our thoughts, feelings and actions relate to each other, that we are totally in integrity within.

You know, simple things like, what you say is what you do. All the sayings lead by example. Well, the thing is we can display the right actions, say the right things but if the feelings inside do not match, and only you know your own feelings, then there is no integrity.

You know like saying yes when you mean no. You do it but maybe you feel resentful inside. That is not a balanced relationship. When we recognize that to be truly in integrity is when we acknowledge that we are not always in integrity. Then we are in integrity. A shaman says that we are always fully negotiable but uncompromising and when we say this we mean we do not compromise our inner balance. We strive to walk impeccably in our lifetime living the way of peace.

The depth to which this takes us individually is a challenge. Every step is about creating a balanced relationship within so that we can begin to create a balanced harmonious relationship with the world around us on every level of our lives.

Now I know that it can start to sound a bit far-fetched and heavy; what I can tell you is that what in fact happens is we learn to take ourselves more lightly. We don't take things so personally anymore and this makes a huge difference in how we see and experience the world.

So how does shadow happen?

What does this mean exactly?

There is so much material on the shadow and shadow work. Here is my understanding of how it works.

The first step:

We are born a bundle of energy 360% of wholeness

Sometimes we have begun to dismantle our wholeness even before we are born.

Immediately we begin to learn what does and doesn't work in relation to this life we find ourselves in. We discover there are parts of our 360% selves that don't work either in our family, friends, society or culture. So we begin to dismantle ourselves, putting those parts of ourselves away in bags that we then carry around with us.

Shadow

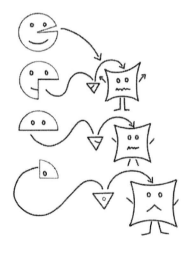

360 Whole – Although some say we already are hiding stuff before we are born

Personal Bag – In our personal bag we put things like Selfishness, anger, beauty, intelligence, spiritual, vulnerable, strength, bitch, weak, beautiful

Society Bag – In our society bag we put: Violence, arrogance, being a woman, being a man,

In our cultural bag we put Red means danger or red means abundance. Beliefs based on certain religions different from your own. You must not step over the line. You cannot be different.

For example:

97

So we end up with three bags full of parts of us and we are left with our persona, our identity that fits and works in this world we find ourselves in.

Our Identity

The trouble is all those things in the bags don't go away. We spend all our time and energy carrying them around ensuring that none come out to be seen and it is exhausting keeping everything hidden. No wonder we sometimes feel too tired to show up for living life today.

On top of this our identity (persona) doesn't want us to change anything because if we do what might happen? This is the only part we have left and it will go out of its way to ensure that we don't change a thing. Why? Because if we start to reclaim other parts of our self this very small part of us will no longer be in charge and we may even begin to recognize that we are beautiful, intelligent, sexy, a bitch, or arrogant. Then what?

So to keep everything comfortable we just keep pushing the other stuff down, deeper and deeper into our sacks, hoping that no one will find out who we really are. The further we push this stuff away and down into the depths of our bags and the longer it is in the bag, this characteristic, this part of us regresses, so that when we do attempt to open our bag it appears savage, so reinforcing our reasons for keeping it there. What we don't realize is that what we try to hide and the more we try to hide it, the more it can be seen and the more likely it is that this banished part of us will sneak past us and turn up in the most inappropriate moments causing the most inappropriate behaviour.

I like to think of it as my personal ketchup bottle. You know at first sometimes the sauce is a bit dense and does not come out easily, so you give it a shake and then if not you give it a tap on the bottom of the bottle and if you are not careful it comes out in one huge splurge, making a mess and ruining a perfectly good meal. I will just add here that it may ruin the meal but depends on how much ketchup we like and if we like a lot of ketchup (drama) in our lives it may just be seen as the payoff for keeping that part of ourselves hidden, reinforcing our story and beliefs about ourselves and our lives.

This is how shadows can turn up, suddenly without warning and making a mess, hurting or ruining something we hold dear to us, relationships, jobs, abundance, love, the list goes on and on. You name it, shadows can sabotage us in any corner of our lives. Until that is we acknowledge it and bring it out of the bag. Once seen, the power of the shadow is reduced. All the time it is locked away it just gets bigger and more volatile likely to show up without warning and that is scary. All these parts of us that we will not or feel we cannot accept still exist, they do not just disappear. Locked away and considered detrimental believe me some time, some place they will be.

Like the story of Dr Jekyll and Mr Hyde is an extreme example of how someone extra nice cannot hold back the part that is really not very nice, until the part that is not so nice turns up and causes harm. And shadows can do this; it can cause harm either to us or to others.

It is not possible to be nice all the time. We can all be nice but we have to remember the times when we are not so nice and maybe this is not to others but this is the internal voice directed at ourselves. Unless we acknowledge and honour the other side of ourselves and bring it into a place of equality with the side we show the world it will make a mess somewhere, sometime.

When we acknowledge these parts of ourselves, it does not mean that we will behave or become the very characteristic. We free up our own energy used to keep it hidden and effectively we begin to become more whole.

Jung said, 'I would rather be whole than perfect'.

We begin to realize that we all have all the potential for all human characteristics within us. Tough one I know but please read on. Try this exercise (originally from *The Dark Side of the Light Chasers* by Debbie Ford)

Name three people you dislike and the characteristics of each one that drive you mad or you really don't like. This can be someone you know, someone famous or a cartoon character.

1

2

3

Now write down the names and characteristics of three people who inspire you.

1

2

3

Take a moment to look at the characteristics and ask where you may have been, are, or could be like this in the future.

I know, I know, there are those of you saying NEVER! I would never be like that. You're right, you may never act like that towards someone else but how about towards yourself? Most of the nasty stuff we do to ourselves, just listen to your internal voice occasionally.

Here's an example.

A number of years ago, a colleague came up to me after a meeting really moaning about another colleague, a manager. I asked what it was that upset her, and she explained that she found this person arrogant, full of all the answers, not willing to listen to anyone else.

So I asked, "Okay, so where in your life might you behave in this way?"

"I don't," she replied. "I have never been like that."

"Okay," I said, "maybe consider the possibility of when you might behave like that."

She huffed and walked away. A few days later, my colleague came up to me and said, "I got it, I got what you meant. I realized that every night before I go to bed I think about all the ways I know would make a better world. I have all the answers. No need to ask anyone else, I've got it. I know it is not a work environment but the attitude is the same, even though I initially did not see it that way. How arrogant that I think I know how to sort the world."

After the next meeting we looked at each other and smiled. "How was that?" I asked.

"Well," she said, "you are not going to believe this, but I was calm and he asked my opinion, for the first time. How mad is that!"

Yes it is bonkers and this is how it works. It sounds simple and yet demands that we look at ourselves without our rose-tinted glasses. If we have a shadow then we have to project this outward to enable us to see it. There is nothing wrong with projecting, we are all doing it. It is how long we leave the projection out there that counts. How quickly we can recognize the part of us that is playing out and bring it back to us is the important work we do. A projection coming back at us normally evokes a reaction. If we take an emotional scale, because being human this is where we spend most of our lives, in the level of emotions, every day we are functioning, let's say on a scale of 0 to 10.

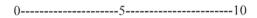

0---------------------5-----------------------10

Let's say on an average day we stay at the level of five, feelings and emotions are there. Our feelings are moving, they come and go, they are light and we transcend them quickly. Emotions are heavier and hang around for longer.

If we suddenly find ourselves in a situation, and I mean any average daily encounter, and we are suddenly overreacting, behaving completely out of proportion in emotions and thoughts and actions to the event, then we have a shadow showing up giving us the opportunity to see it.

This can be an overreaction of any kind; emotional, physical, spiritual or the other end, no reaction at all when we just check out completely.

So a word on reaction.

REACTION is a re-enactment of something that has happened in the past so we use old behaviours based on old beliefs based on past experiences, most of which keep us from seeing the shadow that is right in front of us so that we can continue to blame someone else out there.

It may be that the encounter that we face has triggered a memory in our computer banks that perhaps we don't even remember and we begin to behave in odd or unusual ways that even we do not understand. It can be the encounter has triggered an old pattern and our mind goes back through our computer files to establish how we dealt with and survived this situation the last time. We may not even remember or be aware of the origin of this memory but our mind being very organized has it filed away somewhere for reference. This is when we suddenly find ourselves behaving in a way unknown to us. Or we recognize the behaviour but the reaction is seen as normal and one that our identity would rather we held on to.

There is nothing wrong with feelings. We are all human and that is part of what it means to be human. As I have indicated earlier, feelings move through us, it is what we do with our emotions that make the difference. You may not verbally abuse anyone outside but you may well do it to yourself. So one way or another we harm ourselves or others or both.

There are many schools of thought relating to free expression. I am no psychologist. To acknowledge and honour our emotions, our shadows, beliefs and patterns through ceremony means that we are actively participating in making a shift. Ceremony can be through art, dance, an altar, and mandorlas and can be very beneficial.

If, however, we allow the emotion to bubble over and be expressed from the place it was created the emotional charge can be so strong that it creates electrical pathways in our brains, creating a pattern, an imprint or triggering an existing imprint that then comes online.

Any encounter that causes an over the top reaction is there to teach us something. And this is not teaching us to blame others but to find what it is within us that demanded that this situation occurred in the first place. You see if we take a moment to consider the human psyche, and I am no expert, our identity, the part that we have left, is like a loyal friend, and all the behaviours and beliefs that we have running are deemed by this part of us to be essential to our survival. So the moment a situation arises we want to remember it is an opportunity to ask 'what is this encounter showing me?' Until we acknowledge whatever it is, we will keep creating the same kind of situations and encounters, behaving in the same way because it got you through the last time and it will do again, even if the outcome is horrible. There is a saying: 'you can never get enough of what you don't really want'.

Up until now I have spoken about shadow as negative but shadow is also our positive aspects that we will not accept. We project our magnificence, our intelligence, beauty, and creativity onto others. Why do you think we have actors, actresses, pop stars? There has to be somewhere for us to project our greatness and this can easily be a friend or colleague. Imagine how it would be if you were to acknowledge that part of you, what might it be like?

There is a beautiful writing by Marianne Williamson that Nelson Mandela used in his inaugural speech; it goes like this:

'Our deepest fear is not that we are inadequate

Our deepest fear is that we are powerful beyond measure.

It is our light, not our darkness, that most frightens us.

We ask ourselves, who am I to be brilliant, gorgeous, talented, fabulous?

Actually, who are you not to be?

You are a child of God. Your playing small doesn't serve the world.

There's nothing enlightened about shrinking so that other people won't feel insecure around you.

We are all meant to shine, as children.

We are born to make manifest the glory of God within us.

It's not just in some of us, it's in everyone.

And as we let our own light shine, we unconsciously give other people permission to do the same.

As we are liberated from our own fear, our presence automatically liberates others.'

Often this is more uncomfortable than acknowledging that we are lazy, arrogant, angry etc. We are normally better at acknowledging our characteristics judged as bad rather than those deemed good. But whether you deem them to be good or bad, light or dark, they are all a part of you, you have to know something to recognize it. Remember this. The more you acknowledge and know yourself without any deception, the more energy you will have, the more integrity and balance you will know in your life, and in the world you create. Here is a quote that highlights this beautifully. These are not my words.

'When you meet anyone, remember it is a holy encounter. As you see another, you will see yourself. As you treat another, you will treat yourself. As you think of another you will think of yourself. Never forget this, for in another, you will find yourself or lose yourself.'

I remember when I was training I would regard Alberto and the other teachers and think how amazing they were and that I could never be like them. No matter how many courses I took, how much training, I would never be such a great facilitator. Well I can tell you, as I began to step into the role of facilitator I created more than one occasion when I proved myself right and it was horrible. Until that is I realized that I was never going to be like any of these wonderful people, I could only ever be me, and share from my own journey and my own experiences. Then I got it, I took back my projections, my shadows and my fears and got on with the job and the feedback was amazing even though sometimes it was and still is hard to believe. That is how old habits and behaviours are; they come and knock at the door occasionally and say, "Hi remember me?" and when I am awake I respond, "Yes and thanks for showing me how to share what I have experienced, for showing me the best I can do is be authentic."

The more you acknowledge and know yourself without those rose-tinted glasses and that self-deception, the more energy you will have, the more integrity and balance you will know in your life and in the world you create. Believe me, it does work.

Here's a recap of how it works energetically through the eyes of a shaman. You have a physical body and an energetic body. In the eyes of a shaman all this heavy outdated stuff sits in our energy body just like icons sit on the screen of your computer. Now if one day a situation arises and triggers one of these computer banks or clicks on the icon you suddenly find yourself acting out in a certain way; perhaps that you have never witnessed before and you cannot understand why. It is simply because the icon is open, taking up the whole screen or playing out in your energy field. And when this happens it continues to attract you to situations in an effort to help you to see it and clear it. Once you have cleared the icon then your computer screen goes back to normal. Your life resumes but this time it is different; your vibration has changed because you have more energy available to you, just like your computer may be quicker because it does not have so many programs running.

When we take off our rose-tinted glasses and see ourselves truly without deception, it is I can tell you an eye-opening experience, challenging and incredibly liberating. All the energy bound up in keeping us stuck in that icon, that screen, that pattern is now available and serves our potential for participating in living our life.

I have said it once, maybe twice, and will probably say it again and again. Awareness is the key and using tools that help us take what we discover about ourselves to a place of ceremony, a place of art, gives us the opportunity to bring much more out of our bags than we could ever do by just thinking or talking it through.

So you already are aware of the nature painting and this can be used when looking at our shadows; again taking the situation, and everything that we make it mean, to the mythic is a much easier place to begin to move away from an old way of being towards something more fulfilling.

Mandorla

This is also a great place to introduce you to a mandorla. A mandorla is an ancient symbol that offers a place of reconciliation and hope for the conflicts that we find ourselves facing in our everyday lives.

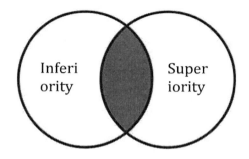

The word mandorla is Italian for almond and represents the almond shape at the centre of two overlapping circles. It is an ancient symbol found throughout the world and represents the union of opposites like masculine and feminine. The symbol appears in images of many cultures around the world and ancient images are thought to represent the mysterious feminine aspect of life – the womb as the portal or doorway between the realm of spirit and of matter.

One of the most famous images is found at Chalice Well in Glastonbury, England. Early Christians understood the symbol to represent the union of Heaven and Earth and used it when they greeted each other. One person would trace a curved line or circle and the other would follow with another, which would overlap in the centre. This almond shape carried a hidden message to communicate a new kind of spirituality. Later it was used as a halo to illustrate the union of spirit and body and can be found in many images depicting Jesus Christ and Virgin Mary and others considered enlightened and holy. These ancient artists honoured the sacred feminine as Mary was depicted in the mandorla as often as Jesus. The symbology enables the coming together of aspects from all cultures, religions and faith. It is a stable container where there is the possibility for spirit to flourish and grow in multiple ways.

So when we create a mandorla we are moving beyond the conflict caused by two opposing sides, so we move away from thinking we have to choose 'this or that', 'either or'. We bring ourselves into the centre where the force of the two sides coming together creates possibility for something new to emerge. It is a symbol of acknowledging and honouring two sides, knowing that the gold, the treasure, is found in the centre where the two opposing forces collide and become one. By bringing them into a form of art, it allows us to be with the coming together, to sense the moment of surrender when a light appears, an idea and a possibility for reconciliation. For a thought, a feeling and an action to emerge, serving an outcome more greatly than continuing the opposing forces and all that these create: conflict, blame, judgment, etc. It allows us to feel inside to observe our internal landscape without causing ourselves or others harm. It can assist us to come to a place of harmony within.

Symbolically the mandorla shows us that the whole has the potential for something greater than the sum of all its parts and this creates possibility. We begin to come back to our centre and understand and acknowledge the principle teaching that we can achieve 'power with' rather than 'power over'.

The mandorla is a mythic way of representing staying centred as we walk a path between opposites, the duality that we experience in our everyday lives. It is a place where we can bring balance to our contradictory human qualities. We bring ourselves to a place which inspires us to think, feel and act from a place of courage, collaboration, sustainability and compassion.

We can use this for addressing issues in our everyday lives and just like the nature painting it allows us to move out of the cold facts of Serpent and emotions of Jaguar and come to the place of the mythic held by Hummingbird. First we open sacred space and then with our intention set clearly we begin to step into the mythic, creating our mandorla.

First we create the two circles so that they overlap and we have the almond shape in the middle. In one circle you place an object in the centre to represent you in the moment and in the other circle you place an object representing the shadow part or projection as you have experienced it. So for example you may have you in the left-hand circle and you may have bully in the right-hand circle. Or you may put victim in one and bully in the other. Then as with the nature painting you take burnable objects and, focusing on your energy, find the thoughts and emotions, behaviours and images and blow this energy on the objects and place them in the relevant circle. So the experiences you have had and your perception of yourself as victim, for example, and then your experiences and perception of bully, or maybe the other way round. Maybe you are doing the bully.

Then, just as with the nature painting you allow this to work out in nature, you allow the invisible world to begin to work with you on an energetic level. Over the next few days go back to your mandorla and notice how you feel, move things if you feel you want to move them. Or you may notice that things have moved anyway. The idea is to gradually come to a place when the two objects representing you in both circles come to the centre almond shape. And as this occurs, be open to the possibility of something new emerging, a possibility for a new way of being. A coming together of the conflict within you can bring the possibility for a peaceful resolution not only on the outside, but more importantly on the inside.

This can be used for a decision that you have to make, personal or business, a choice between two paths. Here you may decide to place an object representing you in the centre almond shape and the feelings and thoughts about the choices in each circle. Again working in a mythic and energetic place there is less definition so we become more open to possibility and see far more opportunity than if we remain with our blinkered vision based on our tightly defined perception of the world.

The best way is to have the experience for yourself. I use this a lot when working with shadow and the shifts and insights can be challenging but incredibly liberating.

A Summary of How Shadow Works

First – we exile all the parts of ourselves that do not fit into our life into a number of bags and we use a lot of energy carrying them around with us.

Second – then in order to see them we have to project them out either onto another person, an organization and so on.

To know that we're projecting we just have to look at our reactions and listen to our language, either internal or external. Remember everyone we talk about, whatever it is about them that we love or hate, we are talking about ourselves.

Rattle

We project, we all do, it is the only way we can see ourselves. Except that we can and do use it to fool ourselves so that we can continue blaming others or pointing the finger at others for what is wrong or right.

Somewhere we have decided that it is easier to continue to blame another than it is to own that which is truly ours. But acknowledging ourselves in our totality can take us to deep and meaningful places, challenging places.

It is when the projection begins to rattle on the face of another that our identity starts to play all sorts of games to keep us from taking the projection back and therefore keeping us from seeing and acknowledging our shadow so we keep our bags.

Let's take an example.

As a young woman working in the banking industry I encountered a man who I perceived as a patriarchal male, in fact a bully, and even though I am a woman both these aspects are a part of my energy also. This man does a very good job of holding this shadow for me. I see him as patriarchal and he demonstrates this in his behaviours. Well that is my perception.

Then I decided that I can stand this no longer and I decide to change jobs. I say good riddance to this man but unknown to me he has exchanged contracts with my next boss who is also a man, handing him the shadow of patriarchal male. So my old boss suddenly feels lighter and my new boss a little heavier.

Suddenly I start to see those patriarchal traits I saw in my old boss now turning up in my new boss. Never saw them before. Remember this is my projection.

I accuse my boss of changing and behaving just like my old boss, but not to his face. Then one day I notice that actually he is not always patriarchal, in fact he is understanding and kind. Now my projection is rattling because if it is not my boss who is patriarchal or bully, then who is it? I go out of my way to change my behaviour to ensure that my new boss keeps the projection. I make mistakes, stay out at lunch late to ensure I get that reaction to confirm that my boss is a patriarchal male bully.

Anything to keep the mask on him, rather than owning that part of myself.

If this does not work then I may find someone else to throw it onto. I will find someone else to hold this projection for me because it cannot possibly be me!

So until I own this part of me, I will continue to encounter men, probably, who will behave in a manner that fits with my perception and projection of a patriarchal male; maybe another male boss, a neighbour, a friend's husband.

Just for the record I recognized my projection and also that I had created a dynamic where I considered myself the victim of my boss, who was the bully. When I realized what I was doing I took back my bully, I recognized that it is not something I do to others but that I constantly did to myself. The next time my boss did act in this way, I stood my ground in an assertive way, I did not attack him or make him wrong. I shifted the level at which I engaged with him and our whole relationship shifted for the better. No longer was I the victim and no longer was he the bully with his patriarchal ways. We found a place where we communicated and worked in a place of service and it was so much easier to go to work. But in order to shift this dynamic it was me who had to own my stuff around the relationship and it is true he could have continued to act in the way he always had done purely to serve the pattern, the beliefs that perhaps we both held. But the encounter was a gift and finally I got my part in the whole play.

We hear about this rattling in circumstances when someone famous or a guru has behaved contrary to what they say or represent. After the shock of realizing the person is human, often we will go out of our way to justify the behaviour in order that the guru can keep the mask or projection of guru and we do not have to own our own version of guru, whatever guru means for us individually.

One thing I love about shaman training is that as we go around the medicine wheel we arrive in the north. In the north we get to a point when we honour and let go of our teachers. This is done to assist us to acknowledge that we are all teachers and that our shaman teachers are also human. And if we keep them on a pedestal they will one day disappoint us. For they are human and like all of us make mistakes and have a journey of self-discovery to accomplish.

Moral intelligence is essential to us and the shaman remind us that we all have stewardship over all of life and that life is sacred.; Without this knowledge goodness knows what kind of world we would live in. However, in some cases we use moral intelligence, that can be personal and subjective to keep the projection exactly where we want it and that is rarely at home with us.

Finally though there comes a moment when we break eye contact with the exterior and at that moment a light occurs that asks us to whom this projection belongs. This patriarchal male or this guru or whatever our projection may be. We may feel a moment of sadness which, if we have the courage to stay with it, helps us to realize it is an awareness of the loss of a part of ourselves, a part of our 360% selves, our energy. We may not like it, but it is ours. Here we can take the decision to leave the shadow out there or we can choose to acknowledge our shadow to become more whole and balanced.

Winston Churchill once said, "I have had to eat many of my own words and I have found the diet quite nourishing."

When we acknowledge our shadow we become more condensed, more centred. Remember the symbol of the mandorla, the two sides coming together. We have more energy available, we are more awake and more aware in our everyday lives. It does not mean we start to become like that particular aspect. What it means is that the energy of that aspect of ourselves is available to us. Sometimes, for example, bitch energy can help get things moving, get things done quickly. It does not mean we behave like a bitch, but rather than using our energy to hide this part of us and projecting it onto someone else, the energy available enables us to get something positive done, something essential, instead of wasting energy continuing to encounter people who we perceive because of our projection as bitches.

So we participate by bringing ourselves into harmony, by reconciling the conflicts that occur within us. This way we stop throwing the conflict out into the world. Equally if we do nothing, after we have recognized the shadow but are passive and refrain from acknowledging and nourishing ourselves, that energy is still out there whether you think you're passive or not. The anger, the bitch, the great and mighty, the weak and poor, abuser, creator are still out there and someone will scoop this energy up and use it to chuck at some unsuspecting individual, society, culture or country. It is powerful and highlights the knowledge of the shaman that we all have a direct influence on the world we experience as we are all interconnected energetically. And unless we take charge of our life and clear our back yards then we will continue to encounter this energy in our lives and in the world that we create.

The fact that we live in a world of duality means that there is conflict. So bringing the two sides together brings us to a centre place of surrender where a higher wisdom can become present. This is our journey with our own shadows.

Be peace, be harmony; sounds easy? It demands personal effort; a journey, as the shaman say, to walk as luminous warriors with no enemies in this world or the next. The more effort we put into this the less likely we are to step onto or stay on the triangle of disempowerment.

The Triangle of Disempowerment

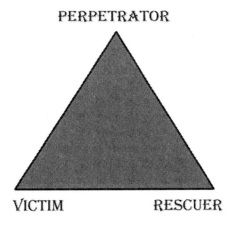

PERPETRATOR

VICTIM   RESCUER

Triangle of disempowerment is a great visual aid to help us to see and to bring into awareness when we play certain roles that are driven by shadow and all the patterns and beliefs wrapped up in them.

The roles of perpetrator, victim and rescuer fuel and nourish each other and getting off this triangle can be a challenge because the payoff of the perceived prize for staying on is greater than the reasons for stepping away.

Each role has energy around it, a feeling, and words.

Victim – poor me, why me, everyone, everything the world is against me, poor me.

Perpetrator – the one who deals the blow (often to ensure that we don't end up the victim, but we do) verbally, physically, emotionally.

The rescuer – the knight in shining armour – DANAH!

I'll save you; I know what will fix you and your life!

The trouble is each role keeps the other role from moving. So each keeps the other in its place, or what simply happens is we all take turns at each role.

This dynamic plays out in our family, our friends, organizations, work colleagues, our society and our cultures and within us.

I had a client whose mother played the victim, blaming her sister for where she was and my client was the rescuer.

So here's how it played out.

Client gets a call from Mum moaning about her sister. My client listens playing the rescuer but as she listens she perceives that her sister has become the victim of her mother so the two swap places. My client stays the rescuer.

As my client did her own work around why she played the role of rescuer on this triangle she began to not participate in the drama and refrained from engaging with the moaning and blaming of her sister. Because she stopped being the rescuer what happened? Her Mum attempted to make her the perpetrator and her sister swapped roles and became the rescuer. The first few times my client found herself pulled back on to the triangle despite her best endeavours to stay off. She looked deeply at her beliefs and behaviours and shifting internally she eventually had the strength to step off and stay off. She found relief, confidence and understanding. Her Mum and sister stayed on the triangle. Her Mum was so determined to remain as the victim she pulled her brother onto the triangle and he became the new rescuer and they all continued to dance around the triangle.

The shaman says that when we have the capacity to step off, for a moment everyone has the opportunity to do the same. If they choose to stay on there is nothing we can do about it. We cannot make anyone else step off, we shift the dynamic by shifting our vibration by way of our behaviours and beliefs and for a moment it creates a pause in the dynamic for others to see themselves clearly but as I have explained we will go out of our way to ensure that the projection stays out there and that we keep our rose-tinted glasses.

Remember there may well be a payoff, a hidden benefit for someone to continue to play a particular role on this triangle of disempowerment. Maybe staying the victim my client's mother believed she would keep her family close. The sad thing is that often it does the opposite. Shadow often gives us more of what we don't really want.

Maybe staying on the triangle as the perpetrator stops our vulnerability from being seen. Usually the bully is a cover for fear or weakness or purely the way we have been influenced in our early lives, this is how to survive life. The bully is usually scared. Scared of what we cannot know but by staying as the bully at least you won't be the victim. Well that is what you think but internally you are a victim of your own shadow.

This triangle happens all around us, at home, with friends, at work. It happens everywhere, country-to-country, culture-to-culture and will continue to do so until we recognize what drives and keeps us on this disempowering dynamic.

Shadow keeps us on this triangle and fear drives our shadows. There are also elements that come from the past through generational beliefs and patterns, things we don't even know that we do not know!

Even karmic stuff, if I dare mention the possibility (if you believe in past lives), if not then stories that live within us.

The Main Causes of Negative and Heavy Energy

The shaman recognizes that there are a number of triggers that can fuel negative energy and cause disease or imbalance in our energy field and in our lives. These revolve around fear, fighting, feeding and sex. They include:

Fear – blame, victim, protection, defensive, controlling.

Fighting – power, money, judging, I'm right you're wrong.

Feeding – envy, jealousy, scarcity, abundance.

Sex – lust, desire, abuse, bigger and better.

A note here: desire is the need to add something to ourselves in order to be our self more fully, except that we see this more in the way of our possessions than our internal being. You know that pair of shoes you just have to have because then you will feel better about yourself. And you can't get them out of your mind until you have them, even if that does mean you have no cash left for the food shopping. And what do they give us; a few moments of pleasure until we move on to the next thing. The commodity industry thrives on our need to make ourselves feel good on the outside and of course this thirst is never quenched because the true fulfilment comes from who we are on the inside. What kind of garden we are cultivating on the inside is what matters most. And then fear is about us losing something and therefore becoming diminished and being less. Both these very strong compulsions we have obscure the fact that being cannot be given or taken away. Being in its fullness is already within us. We can still have lovely possessions, a wonderful home, eat good food and we can still aspire to achieve these things in our lives. We realize that they do not define who we truly are. For all these things remain here when we die. So it is the treasures we gain on the inside that we take with us, everything else stays here.

It is true that money is important in our lives. Having some money makes life easier in the world today. However if our focus is purely on making loads of money and only this, then we negate the original intention, because our energy and focus is on the end product defined so tightly we miss opportunities. You see money cannot make you rich or successful. Money requires a number of other relationships to enable it to grow.

And one person's perception of rich is different from another's. Some people may appear poor to us, but they consider themselves rich for a whole number of reasons, whether this be their good health, the environment that they live in, the love of the people around them. So remember that all of us have a perception and a belief about what makes us rich. Certainly I remember a story that Alberto once told of his mentor who described how many who came to the mountains in Peru thought of the mountain people as poor. He explained that the Q'ero have a relationship with the mountains, the rivers, the sky and the natural world that they have stewardship over. As stewards of the land they live upon they live outside of time whereas we in the West own the land and are consequently owned by time. The mountain people do not consider themselves poor, for spiritually they are full up on the inside. Saying this does not mean that they do not have their own shadows to reconcile; we are all human after all.

If you were to imagine money like a river, if your river is representing your relationship with money, how might it look?

Again for example it may be your river is dammed up so is this representative that, like water that is stationary, money has become stagnant, it may break down, deteriorate? It cannot move and so dies. Maybe there is movement but it is a tiny stream with so many obstructions it is a challenge for money to move freely.

I know we can have lots of beliefs around money, some of which I have witnessed and noted below. It is about bringing our relationship with money into balance. We can have loads of money and spend our lives in fear of losing it. You see the fear of losing something that we believe defines who we are can control our life and this is not just material possessions or money it can be our beliefs and our strategies to survive life.

Money is a vehicle on which we project many things. However, money itself is benign, meaning it has no meaning until we put something on it or demand something of it. There are some sayings that are still in use today. You hear them in conversations.

'Money is the root of all evil.' Now there is a school of thought that this comes from the Bible; however the phrase in the Bible reads, 'For the love of money is the root of all evil.' Do you see the difference? It is not money itself that is evil it is our intention that creates the outcome that can be perceived as evil.

This is saying that loving money above God, Spirit or whatever name you give this force is not recommended. Maybe this is the counsel to be aware of. It is our intention behind our use and desire for money. And then who decides what is evil and what is good?

Shakespeare himself said, 'There is no good or evil only thinking makes it so.'

There are other expressions, most of which are negative, like 'filthy rich'. You can imagine if you have been influenced at any point by this kind of expression you may have decided or someone in your family line may have decided that if you are rich you may be seen as being corrupt or to have acted in an underhand way to gain your wealth.

There are many who, through passion for their work and hours dedicated to great causes or simply their jobs, have made a good relationship with money and with value and so are now, from an outsider's point of view, rich. Are they filthy rich? No, they are doing well because they have a relationship with money that represents the value that they bring to the work that they do or have done. Most importantly they began their work with a sense of purpose for the value that they would bring to the role rather than purely making a stack load of money. Maybe they did dream of making a stack load of money and maybe that is how they started out but then realized that in order to create a relationship of integrity with money they had to also manage their relationship with purpose and value.

Yes, I know there are those who make money from other ways that maybe are not in integrity or right relationship. Somewhere down the line this will show up. Believe me.

So here's another belief, all these I share have come up in classes. Maybe way back in your family history someone decided that there wasn't any point in earning or making good money because the lord of the land would take at least half from you in tax. And let's face it, none of us like paying tax but looking at it from another perspective we all demand services and these have to be paid for by something. How the money is spent and whether it is of service to the community depends on the integrity of the people who manage it.

What about the belief 'we have to work for nothing'? Sometimes this crops up in those of us who choose professions seen as therapeutic or healing. Well, if you can truly give your services for nothing in return, I ask you two questions.

Firstly can you truly do this without wanting for anything, and can you not charge without thinking of what you don't have or what you could have if you charged?

You see when we give something away and then spend time thinking about what we have not got then we are out of integrity.

In my opinion, and it is only my opinion, it is far better to charge for the service, for two reasons. One, you bring yourself into alignment, there is value in what you do and how you behave, and secondly, the person you are assisting will value your time and will commit themselves to the process of their own healing journey. Remember a shaman is always looking at the relationship. Our lives are about creating right relationships; if we work for nothing then all kinds of internal emotions can arise. I have seen in my practice, by there being no exchange the client either sees you as the powerful one and always feels like they are in a place of debt, (you may like this!) or there may be a sense from the client's perception that there is no value in the work you do. These are just a few examples of issues that have arisen during classes and I feel are worth sharing here.

There is a wonderful story of the fisherman who lives very simply, he uses his boat to take people across the river and when he is not doing this he catches fish for his supper. Except what he does with his fish is cut off its head, keeps this for himself and gives the body of the fish away to the people he helps across the river. He asks for nothing in return.

He has an apprentice and one day he asks his apprentice to go to his mentor and ask what it is that he is missing. He knew that something was not going well with his spiritual growth, he felt he had come to a place where he could not move further forward.

So the apprentice made the journey to the mentor and was surprised to find that the mentor was very wealthy, he lived in a wonderful home with plenty of food and riches.

The apprentice explained the situation of his own mentor (the fisherman) and could not believe it when the rich mentor said, "The problem is that the fisherman gives the best part of the fish away."

What! The apprentice could not believe what he was hearing. "What do you mean; surely this is a selfless thing to do?"

But the wealthy mentor said no more and asked the apprentice to return to the fisherman with his message. When the apprentice arrived he came to his own mentor and relayed the message. The fisherman sat for a moment and sighed. "Ah! Now I see, yes I give the fish away and this appears like a selfless thing that I do, a gesture of my inner work. But it is true when I am eating my fish head, all I can think about is how good the rest of the fish must taste!"

This wonderful story is an example of saying and doing things with integrity, also highlighting that the fisherman's spiritual mentor recognized that his wealth did not define who he was on the inside. He could not be defined by his material possessions nor was he attached to his material wealth. Whereas the fisherman appeared to be acting selflessly but was attached to the very thing he had given away, the part of the fish he did not have. If he had been able to cook and eat his fish head with gratitude without a thought of what he was missing or did not have then he had the possibility to be liberated and available for wealth. Integrity is an important subject in shamanic training as we are always looking to create a place within us that is honest, humble, whole and unified.

I learned very quickly that as I came into integrity with this aspect of myself then the people who came to me would truly want to commit to their own journey. They are not looking for a quick fix, but a journey of self-discovery that will bring them to a place where they participate fully in their life. And if I ever hold a space for someone and do not charge, I really check inside with myself first for I know if there is an inkling of discontent within me then this will permeate into the relationship.

So where do we focus? Do we focus on what we do not have or do we focus on what we do have? It is said that energy flows in the direction that we put our intention. This is true but if we have an underlying belief system that we are not aware of, a belief that continues to sabotage our attempts to build a beneficial relationship with money then no attempt will work until, that is, we discover what we truly believe and shift it.

So how is your relationship with money?

I want you to take a moment to meet with money. You see today our relationship with money is diluted because most of us see money as plastic. We get cash from a machine with a plastic card and a lot of us, not all of us, use plastic to do our shopping. A lot of us as a result of using plastic know money as debt.

So here is an opportunity to take five minutes to get a sense of your own relationship to money.

Take the largest denominator of money that you have; a note is better for this exercise if you can, but if you only have a coin then this is okay. Now holding the money that you have in your hand, take a good look. Notice the colours, the pictures, the texture and the smell. Take a moment to really be with the physical manifestation of money that you have in your hands.

Notice how your body feels. Are there any sensations or fears? What feelings or heavier emotions are you experiencing? And where are you experiencing these in your body? Take space to notice. Remember money is benign; it only takes on the persona that we give it.

Now, taking a couple of deep breaths, close your eyes and go inside your body. Notice your body and with every exhalation give your body an opportunity to relax just a little more.

Then take a deep breath and imagine you are gathering all the distractions, aches, pains and thoughts into an imaginary bubble and bring that bubble to the area of your heart and release with a big sigh. We call this the breath of surrender.

Now more relaxed, I would like you to imagine that you are walking along a path, notice the landscape the smells, colours, sounds and feelings that you have as you take this walk. You are holding the money in your hand.

As you follow your path it begins to widen out and you find yourself in a beautiful meadow; bright radiant grass and flowers welcome you, together with the sound of birds. This place is fully alive and flowing with the universe.

You notice just in front of you a place to sit and you make your way over, maybe there is a seat here or maybe it is a lovely patch of moss, soft and velvety to sit on. If you are not getting anything I invite you to open your imagination; what might it be like? Now you are comfortable, you are going to call upon the energy of money that lives within you. You are going to invite money to come and sit with you.

This is an invitation and an acknowledgement of this energy in your life. Allow a few moments for this energy to show itself. How does money look to you? Does money have a sound, a voice, a tune? What may be wrapped around this energy? Maybe it is bound, maybe it seems very controlled or completely out of control. Notice how the energy appears to you and notice what is happening inside your body as you do so.

Breathe deeply, releasing any tension that may arise. Acknowledge money here in this space without any judgment or preconceived ideas. Now ask money how you can work with each other to ensure a balanced relationship. Ask if there are any hidden beliefs that you may not have seen or be aware of. Allow space for everything to be seen. Let money know how much you value the relationship and the opportunity to shift the relationship to a place of balance and value.

Here you exchange a small gift with money, a natural gift from your meadow and money gives you a gift to represent this meeting. This is a way of acknowledging the shift in your relationship. You thank money for showing up and begin to make your way back through the meadow to the path, following the path, sensing the sights and sounds, following the path the way you came until you sense yourself back in your body. Notice the weight of your body on the floor or chair, the sense of the room that you are in. Take a deep breath, wriggle your fingers and your toes.

Stretch your body, breathing in and on the exhalation open your eyes, bringing yourself back fully into the room where you began this journey.

Take a few moments to reflect on your meeting with money and to notice your body. Look at the note or coin that you have in your hand and bringing this up to your mouth, imagining the gift you received from money, blow this gift into the note or coin.

Now taking this note or coin you can create a small altar to honour your new relationship with money. If you feel you want to continue to work with the insights or feelings you have become aware of then you can create a nature painting and release any other thoughts and feelings into the nature painting, being open and willing to new opportunity and possibility within this relationship.

Value

This leads me on to how we value ourselves. Value is not something that can be given or taken away. It is not something that you can gain from comparison with others. Value is how you are within and how you bring value to your relationship with the world around you. Value is not about money.

I am sure that we have all experienced times when we have chosen to buy something or pay for some services based on our overall experience rather than just the product. In fact this is how we evaluate value most of the time. It is dependent on thoughts, words or actions experienced during the purchase experience, whether this is for material purchases or other services.

So how do you value your contribution to life on a scale 0 to 10? Write the number quickly now without thinking about it.

Now take a look at the number you have written down and notice what is happening inside, your thoughts, feelings and emotions. We can have so many patterns and beliefs wrapped up around this one subject and often they are not originated by us. Our external influences have a great impact on how we see ourselves in the world. If you have grown up constantly being told you are no good, or you're stupid or weak or useless, etc., it stands to reason that you may well start to believe that this is who you are. It is all in our language. We tend to use the verb to be, for example, "You are a naughty boy."

Well if we say this to a child often enough he may decide that he cannot be anything else but naughty because that is who he is. He is not naughty, his behaviour is naughty – there is a difference.

And yet through habit I know myself in the everyday I slip back into this language pattern instead of being awake enough to clarify the actions and not the person. It is so important that each one of us realizes that we all make a contribution however large or small to the evolution of life on this planet and so therefore we are all, every single one of us, of value in this great play we call life.

You don't see ants doubting their value in their colony. Each and every one of those ants knows it has an important part to play in the longevity and welfare of its world. So no matter what task, role or job you play, know that it does matter and your relationship within this is of value. When we undermine another persons' value of themselves, we have to look at why we do this and then remember that this affects us all. We all want to belong to something, to find our place in the world. We're human, remember, and we will gravitate to those places that we perceive value us. Again we have to recognize that this external search is futile unless we have accepted our value on the inside. The internal value that we hold for ourselves is the part that will stand us strong throughout our life.

We have been through years where individualism has been portrayed as a good thing, but my sense is it is not natural to us humans. We thrive in community, wanting to belong is part of being human. As teenagers when we are doing our best to deal with hormones and the stages of becoming an adult, valuing ourselves and knowing that we are valued is crucial to how we will evolve both in our lives and how we will assist the evolution of society and life on this planet. And this really applies to us all. For a moment I focused on our teenage years because this is, I sense, when we are most vulnerable to be gobbled up by causes that may not be seen as favourable but do offer us a sense of purpose and value. This is where community has an opportunity to be there to support young people through challenging times.

So here you have an opportunity to use the existing nature painting from your exercise with money or you can create a new nature painting, or even a mandorla if you sense this is a better tool for you to use right now. Look at your score and how you value yourself. Create your circle and blow any thoughts, feelings, emotions that come as a result of this internal enquiry. Acknowledge and honour all that shows up. You may have emotions you were not expecting, let them be seen; remember lots may be linked to old patterns and outmoded behaviours and beliefs. Take this opportunity to shift your own map, shift your perception of yourself. What little thing can you do each day to remind yourself that you are of value? And do it.

When we have the courage to transcend our old beliefs and ways of being, we no longer have to keep living from places that fuel the key triggers for disease.

Fear

Fear is a learned response; there is an acronym.
FALSE
EXPECTATIONS
APPEARING
REAL

Fright on the other hand is instinctual and necessary to keep us from danger.

We live in a society, a world that is driven by fear. We are always being told how scared we should be, what we should be fighting. There is a sense that we are always under attack and there is never an all-clear signal.

My dad says during the war in London, when the bombers were coming the sirens would go. Everyone would drop everything and get to a shelter as quickly as possible. The bombers would come; you could hear the devastation, the noise.

Then there would be a siren that gave the all clear. Everyone would come out of the shelters and get to work on the clear up or back to their work.

We see this natural survival instinct in nature where the gazelle is chased by the cheetah. The adrenal glands kick in, the fight or flight reaction activates and the gazelle has the energy to run and run. Once the chase is off and, let's say on this occasion the gazelle escapes, you will see it shake as it lets any excess energy go and it then goes back to grazing.

If you're interested this is how it works physically.

In our brains we have the hypothalamus organ; on the signal of fear the hypothalamus produces corticotropin-releasing factor, which in turn notifies the pituitary gland to release adrenocorticotropic hormones (ACTH) into the blood. This in turn notifies the adrenal glands to activate fight/flight, flooding the system with adrenal hormones. This is known as the HPA axis.

When the HPA axis mobilises stress hormones, it constricts the blood vessels of the digestive tract, forcing oxygen-rich blood into the arms and legs ready for action. So the visceral organs stop life-sustaining work; the digestive, absorption, excretion and other functions that provide for growth of cells and regulate the body's energy reserves are inhibited. This action also represses the action of the immune system to conserve the body's energy and this interferes with our ability to deal with disease. Not only this, but it also interferes with our ability to think clearly.

Our processing of information in the forebrain, which is our centre of reason and logic, is slower than the reflex action, which is controlled by the hind or reptilian brain, as in an emergency this part of our brain processes information more quickly so the organism survives. For example if we were to use our forebrain when a bus was coming towards us, by the time we had reasoned how far away it was and that we had to run to get out of the way, we would already be underneath it. So the reptilian brain does this for us.

The whole mechanism is amazing, just like our body with its innate intelligence always has me in awe. However, whilst the HPA mechanism is brilliant for handling acute stresses, it was not designed to be activated continuously.

In our world today most of the fear stresses are not acute immediate threats. If they were we could identify them, respond and move on. We are constantly faced with supposedly unresolvable worries about our personal lives, jobs, our war-torn globe, terrorists and the weather, to name a few.

Our language is full of nuances that imply some kind of threat, battle or fight. You could be forgiven for perceiving that we should live permanently in a state of fear and yet most circumstances do not threaten our immediate survival. On the contrary, when we are faced with a situation we want the body to have enough energy to be able to respond. If this reaction has been permanently on, then when we do really need it, the body has to draw on even more resources to fulfil the demand.

I remember on one occasion when I was out for the evening with a friend. We went to a local restaurant, had a lovely evening and walked home. It was late and walking home in our town was not a problem, we had done this many times. Except this time as we were walking home, I noticed someone appear behind us. From the corner of my eye, I could see that it was a young man. My friend had not noticed and was busy talking. I decided that I would slow our pace and then the young man could overtake us. But as I slowed down, so did he. At this point I felt my body tense up. I quietly said to my friend we're being followed, keep walking, there is a food store ahead and it's still open so we can go in there if we have to. So we kept walking. As we approached the shop the young man disappeared. We stopped but my body was still tense; something was wrong. We were now on a main road, the shop was just shutting but the kebab shop was open and there was activity so my friend who lived up this road said that she felt okay to walk and I asked her to ring me when she got home.

I, on the other hand, lived much closer to the store but my road was very quiet and dark (at this time there were no street lights).

As I said goodbye to my friend, I caught sight of the young man and another across the road hiding behind a bush. I turned round, my body tensing up even more; I could hear my heart beating, it was so loud. I walked fast, I did not run. I knew they were behind me and all I knew was that I had to get to my door. Here I could either alert a neighbour or get my husband up. I managed to get the key in the door first time in the dark, open and shut the door very quietly. I stayed in the dark for five minutes. My breathing was really heavy. Suddenly the phone rang; I jumped out of my skin, it was my friend. She was home but concerned because as she had walked up the main road she had seen the men run across the road after me. I was ok.

After the phone call I stood up against the wall and started shaking, my whole body shook, just like that gazelle. All that adrenal energy that had accumulated to assist me was being released. I had the all clear, I was ok. The next day I reflected on this encounter to see what I had learned. For me this experience showed me the gift of being aware and awake to those things that happen around us and to know the difference between a perceived threat and a real one.

I learned how my body responds to a real threat, I listen carefully to my body, not my mind. We never get the all-clear signal anymore. So our adrenal fight or flight response can be permanently switched on. If this is the case the body withdraws all its energy from the internal organs so that it has the energy for our limbs to either fight or run. You can imagine over a long period of time without an all clear signal our digestive system, our absorption of the nutrients from our food, our elimination processes begin to slow up or stop all together. Our nervous system becomes depleted. This we see in those of us who have perhaps experienced trauma when very young and due to either the circumstances or not being able to reason that it is okay now our HPA axis has been switched on for years and years. Those caught in the midst of war, famine; internal family situations, social situations. This can affect us detrimentally on all levels if left unchecked.

So if we are always the victims of something out there – how can we get off the triangle?

I remember seeing a notice at a station once, a huge billboard notice that read, 'Join the battle to get our children to read.'

What? Where's the battle? Who's the enemy and how long should we be afraid that there's a battle to fight to get our kids to read?

If everything is a fight or a battle we're saying we are the victim of something or someone. Maybe, just maybe if we begin to recognize encounters not as battles but opportunities and our enemies as adversaries who happen to be part of a situation that offers us a place of reconciliation, then maybe we can shift our own vibration and stop creating the need to keep experiencing these kinds of encounters. Yes, we may still have to make a stand, but not from a place driven by fear and anger. If we continue to act from this place – remember the levels of engagement – all we get is more of the same or worse.

There is a wonderful story from the Q'ero nation.

When the conquistadors came the Q'ero fought for their people, but they did not see the Spanish soldiers as enemies, purely as adversaries who happened to be there like them in this situation. They had no fear of bullets and the Spanish soldiers were scared of the Q'ero fighters because they would fire their guns and it appeared that the bullets would miss. And if a Q'ero fighter killed a Spanish soldier he would cast some of his own blood to acknowledge that had they been together in another time or place; they may have shared stories around a fire. They may have been friends.

What this illustrates is by not having fear of the bullet the very subject of the fear did not reach its target. Legend and lore says that 'what we fear will find us'; we will attract it.

If we can remain fearless, which is not reacting from a place of anger or violence or fear, then there is no triangle of disempowerment so something else is possible. The encounters may still be uncomfortable but maybe without bloodshed, harm and loss of life. The outcome has the possibility of being more of service in the long run for all involved.

We often choose to stay on the triangle in situations and moan and blame purely because it is too scary to consider another way. It is easier to stay with what we know and continue to play the same roles, go around the triangle, because what will happen if we step away? We would rather stay with this old situation because we know it really well and we know how to deal with it even though the outcome is always horrible and never changes, but that's okay because we know it. Even in its discomfort it is more comfortable than stepping away into a new place. Why? Because the outcome is unknown. Even if stepping off means we could live a better life and find a new way of being in our lives. It seems madness that we would choose like this, but I know from personal experience that taking that step takes a lot of courage.

If we have fear of something happening, for example, our beliefs and behaviours will be such that they will, in the long run, create exactly what we do not want.

For example, I was speaking with a Mum who happened to share with me that she was concerned about the relationship she had with her son. She was experiencing him as insolent, rude and aggressive. Now she is a single parent and her first concern is the welfare of her son. Except her son saw her as always on his back, that she didn't have a life so her focus was always on him and she asked too many questions. This was really hurting her and, as we spoke, I asked her what her relationship was like with her own mother. She explained that she felt like she could not be herself so left home. The first two months she was away she did not communicate with her Mum, so her Mum had no idea where or how she was. Now her greatest fear was that her own son would leave in the same manner. She understood that one day he would fly the nest but she really did not want it to be in the same way.

However, do you see? Even though this was her fear, her behaviour was creating the same dynamic with her son as she had with her own Mum. The pattern was directed by the fear and so it was possible that this same scenario would be created yet again. Unless, that is, Mum took the time to look within at her own reasons for behaving in the way that she did, so that she could shift her own beliefs and behaviours; then she had the possibility to establish a new dynamic with her son that was of service to them both. I shared with her some of the teachings around patterns and as we talked she began to recognize things about herself and suggested to me that perhaps when her son came home she would stop asking loads of questions.

We talked about the things that she used to do but now finds it difficult to because of work; looking after her son and resources, money in other words. I asked her to consider the possibility of showing her son that it is possible to have a life even as a single parent. Find something that you love, she mentioned dancing, and said that she would look for a class she could afford. Of course this may not be realistic so I asked her to consider something that maybe did not require money. She loved walking so we agreed that Friday evenings we would meet and go for a walk. Great – the first time we did this we stopped for a glass of wine on the way home. Her son phoned her to ask where she was. You see; she was not at home waiting for him. Things were different. Interesting, isn't it?

As parents we want to take the opportunity to show our children that being a parent does not mean you have no life. I know I am willing to take the opportunity to create a dynamic relationship where my kids feel supported, not enclosed. Yes, the boundaries are necessary and yet we want to always be aware of how these serve everyone in the relationship. Remember we may consider them essential purely because that is all we have ever known in our map and despite the discomfort we find it comforting because we know it. Naturally teenagers want to disassociate from their parents. It is a natural evolution in all our lives as we mature. Depending on the circumstances teenagers sometimes feel the only way to break away is to destroy all that they know and love and this is normally an unconscious act to enable them to feel they can stand alone.

This transition demands that as parents we recognize within us what is running the show and stop blaming our kids or ourselves. The sooner we can come to peace with this evolution within our family the easier it is for everyone. And yet it can be such a challenge to make the shift.

By recognizing her part in the dynamic this wonderful woman realized what had been playing out, and although she admitted it was going to be hard, she would stop asking questions as soon as her son came in the door. She was prepared to make the effort to shift her behaviour and her beliefs. I spoke to her a couple of weeks later and, despite her best efforts, her son's behaviour had become worse. Remember, people will go out of their way to keep things as they were and most of the time this is unconscious. She shared with me how she had reflected a lot on her own behaviour and beliefs and slowly one small change within her behaviour had begun to shift the whole dynamic. She admitted that it was not as easy as she had thought but she could feel that the level at which she was engaging with her son now had the opportunity to shift, creating the possibility for a more balanced relationship. You can see we get so consumed by our roles – here the role of parent or Mum, but there are many and in the process we forget who we truly are, and in the process suffocate the very people we love.

How this works is that when we find ourselves in a dynamic run by a pattern with all its complex parts there is an expectation on how each member will behave. So when we look the fear in the face, shift our beliefs and our behaviour others sense they are in limbo for a moment whilst they try to work out what is different and how they should behave. Here there is an opportunity for them to shift as well if they choose – we cannot make them. And remember, sometimes others' behaviour will become more intense, in order that things stay the same and they can continue to blame you, that you continue to carry the projections. The patterns will demand that everything stays as it is.

Sometimes the shift is so subtle it takes a few hours, days or even weeks to recognize that something has changed. This is how by shifting our energetic vibration we can inform our lives as the shift passes from the energetic to the mythic to the level of beliefs, feelings and behaviours into our daily life. The beauty of working with this knowledge in a shamanic way is that we can shift systems, patterns and beliefs in the place of energy or Eagle, as shaman call it.

Here ninety-nine percent of what we shift is energy and only one percent is matter. You know, physical, material stuff, like emotions.

A person trying to move a whole house. Sweating

A person moving 1 brick. Easy peasy

It is a lot easier than shifting something ninety-nine percent in the material, physical and one percent energetic. Why, it would be like literally attempting to move your house, bricks, mortar and all. You can imagine the amount of energy this would take, let alone money. So you would be inclined to stay in your house where it is because it is easier. I don't blame you, sounds like a good idea to me. Who in their right mind would want to attempt something like that?

The method used by shaman helps to change our vibration (that's energy) and by doing this the shift energetically begins to inform us in our emotional, physical everyday lives. And this in turn aids us to create some new coordinates for our new map to support us as we begin to live in a different way. And this does not necessarily have to be a huge momentous shift. It could be as simple as finally greeting the grumpy guy at the newspaper stand with a cheery smile and walking away without whispering, "What a grumpy old git."

Walking away with a smile means that you have not allowed someone else to tell you how you're going to feel today.

Maybe he is always grumpy and maybe, before, you have muttered grumpy things as you have started your day. Today you can genuinely smile at him, say have a great day and mean it.

So you see I am talking about our lives in any moment. Yes of course there are huge discoveries we can make that bring about a huge light bulb moment and our lives completely change. I am not promising thunderbolts and lightning mind you, just want to make that clear.

The great part is that we start to really participate in our journey and it is incredibly empowering. Being aware of the shadows that drive us, the beliefs and old habitual behaviours that we run assists us to really take charge of our lives. Acknowledging ourselves truly without deception is one of the greatest gifts and legacies we can bring to the world we create.

Knowing that each one of us is here and participating whether we know it or not in reconciling the past and creating the now. I say now because the future is now. How we behave now in this moment influences the world around us, whether we see this as our local world or the global world. Each generation simply is part of the continual evolution of humankind and of the incredible planet that we inhabit.

Disengaging Fight and Flight

There is a way to assist the body to disengage this fight or flight response. It does mean that we have to face our own part in remaining caught in this disempowering way. We may have to look at the story we tell, identify our role within the story, together with our beliefs and expectations. Then begin to release this energy that keeps us stuck by creating a nature painting or asking for assistance. Once we have cleared the energy that keeps the fight or flight response engaged and shifted our perception of the events then we can disengage. If we try to do this before we release the heavy energy responsible for this axis to be activated we may cause more stress to the body. It stands to reason that if you have a strategy and belief still running, your system is not going to want to turn off the power just in case. However, once you have identified and become aware of the energy then in the process of discharging this the fight and flight axis can be rebalanced. We can do this ourselves or with another person that we trust.

First open sacred space, then open your wiracocha; the processes are at the beginning of the book if you need to remind yourself.

Place both your hands under or on top of the body in the area of the heart between the breastbone in the centre. Then feel for or imagine the heartbeat of the earth. This is a slow steady beat. Bring your heartbeat or the heartbeat of your partner to the same rhythm as the heartbeat of the earth.

Once you have this move your left or right hand, depending on what side of the body you are, and place this just below the belly button or in the same area under the back if you are working from underneath. This is close to the level of the adrenal glands.

Then use your hands to act as the bridge informing the adrenal glands from the heartbeat of the earth. This energetically sends a message to the body that it can stop sending the chemicals to the adrenals and the body can relax. If you are doing this on yourself then you will be lying on your back. Place your hands on top of your body and follow the map in the same way.

If we take a moment to remember at the beginning of the book I spoke about the brain in the heart and that it is the heart that informs the brain what the body needs. It also makes logical sense that we would bring the heart to a relaxed state and then transmit this to the body.

An Example of Using a Nature Painting for Shadow Work

Here is another example of using shamanic tools to help shift a family dynamic.

When my first son was born I perceived that my husband was selfish. My experience was a huge shift in my relationship with my husband when our children came along. Of course the map changed, our whole world changed. Anyway the reason I saw my husband as selfish was that after working all week we only had the weekend and he would go out, play football and golf and I would be left at home with the kids. I enjoyed being with my kids, don't get me wrong, but I created a triangle where I made myself a victim of my husband's sports and my kids were my rescuer or my reason for making him the perpetrator. Well, this caused many arguments and uncomfortable stand offs, until I decided that I did not want to play this game anymore. I was fed up with every Saturday or Sunday experiencing a horrible atmosphere. All created by me although I didn't realize it at the time.

So having trained as a shaman I created a nature painting and took a look at why I thought my husband was selfish and then where maybe I was selfish. What I realized was that my husband loved to spend time with the kids but I always had to have control over where they went and what they would do. Selfishly I would let him have time with the kids the way that I wanted him to. I did not like seeing that and it would have been easy to ignore this and keep blaming him for the atmosphere. So I did my personal work around the whole thing, worked it through a nature painting and began to create a new coordinate. Then one Sunday a few weeks later my husband came home late from golf. This time however I had made dinner late so when he knocked at the door, I opened it said, "Hi, you're just in time for dinner, I'm just serving up," and with that I walked back to the kitchen. As I did this I thought, well that was different and smiled to myself. As I looked back at the front door, my husband was still standing there with his golf clubs, looking at me with a strange expression on his face.

"What's up? Quick, you can open the wine," I said.

So he came in, put his golf clubs away and came into the kitchen, very sheepishly. "There's the wine," I said and looked at him. "What's up?" I asked.

"I'm waiting," he replied.

"For what?" I asked

"I'm not sure really but you normally have a go at me, so I am just waiting just in case it has been delayed."

"Okay, but it won't be if you don't open the wine!" I exclaimed, and we both smiled, he opened the wine and we had a lovely meal with the kids. So you see I shifted and the dynamic shifted and for a while my husband did not know how to behave because everything was different to how he expected it to be. Interesting, isn't it? I still smile when I remember that moment looking to see him still standing on the doorstep waiting and wondering what had happened.

So I decided to stop making my husband the perpetrator in our relationship. I had to see myself honestly and by making a shift energetically a moment was created when a different experience was possible. Now you may be still thinking he was selfish and yes, he did continue to play golf and football, but after a while he began to have days at home so we could all go out as a family or I could go out with friends while he had the kids. You see, I no longer selfishly held the rules for how to be with the kids so he was able to spend time with them without me being right behind him all the time. Would you want to spend time with people if you were being watched all the time and told how to be with them? As I shifted it created a possibility for the dynamic to shift and it did and it served us all as a family.

In the shamanic world we never want to use another to heal our own wounds. There is a saying; sorcery or disempowering people happens even when we have the best intentions. And this normally occurs when we see something as needing fixing and we think we know what is needed.

Some further examples to help you get the idea how this works out in our lives.

Recently a friend phoned because there was a situation that had arisen with her granddaughter. My friend wanted to help but she did not know how. She wanted to be there for her daughter. I asked her how she was feeling and her response was that she felt frustrated and helpless. Why, because she did not know how she could help.

I want to point out here; we always think we know how the other person may be feeling. Who really knows? The person themselves and they may not tell you. We had no way of knowing how her granddaughter really felt. My friend had a sense of how her daughter was because they had spoken on the phone.

Now here my friend was experiencing her own helplessness, her own frustration. This was not for her daughter or granddaughter but for her.

She wanted to be a solid rock for her daughter and in order to be that she had to look at her own helplessness and come to terms with this, to bring it into balance, to honour its origins and recognize the feelings without becoming helpless. She had to ask her daughter how she could be of assistance to her.

You see from our own rose-tinted glasses we may think we know what is needed, we may think we know the answer, but we can never know exactly where someone else is or how they are feeling unless they tell us. So if we go in to rescue someone because we mistake our own helplessness for theirs then we can make a mess because we will behave in a way that will not serve the other person; our behaviour, believe it or not, will be to serve us and our own insecurity, our own shadow.

Now my friend is a trained shaman so very quickly she was able to recognize her own stuff, own it and become the rock her daughter needed in that moment. But it is hard. We so want to help others when we see them in challenging and sometimes awful situations.

We can but we want to be of service to them, we do not want to be using their situation in an attempt to heal our own stuff.

That is the depth to which the spiritual work of the shaman takes us. There is never anyone out there to blame and ultimately our aim is to be of service to another. To be of service is not about serving someone (just want to make that clear) it is about being clear and available to assist them to take the opportunity, the challenge, to support them in their journey. We never regard any situation as needing to be fixed or someone as needing rescuing. Why, because in the moment we are saying something is wrong, so in the moment the universe responds to something is wrong rather than to a possibility or opportunity for evolution. (Rescue, here means when we jump in because we think we know what needs to be fixed. We know best.)

However, if I work in the medical or emergency services then when I turn up in my role as a policeman, fireman, paramedic, then I will do what is necessary to fulfil my role for the individual. The shaman say, "You get bitten by a snake, go get the anti-venom first then take the time to find out why you were available to get bitten."

So in some situations action is required, it is a matter of life and death. Then after the immediate action is taken the internal enquiry can take place. "Why was I available for that? What happened? What pattern? What belief?"

Sometimes it is necessary to draw a line in the ground and say that is enough. We have to have firm boundaries for our teenagers to push against. They have to know when their behaviour is not ok. If we are able to maintain a place of balance within and not fight from a place of fear, hatred and anger then we may have cracked it. Now that is our challenge.

As soon as we can bring awareness to our thoughts, feelings and actions (behaviour) then we have the key to make a difference.

This is when we do have a choice, whether we stay with the old, even though it is uncomfortable and we moan about it. Or we choose to take a step in to a new way of being and perhaps step by step begin to experience living our lives differently. As the levels of engagement evolve within us, they enable us to face our fears and daily conflicts more consciously. Serpent reminds us to stay focused on the real issue rather than bringing old histories to the moment. Jaguar reminds us to breathe deeply and stay centred, bringing order from chaos the eye in the storm. Hummingbird reminds us that nothing is personal or wrong. The moment represents an opportunity to grow. Eagle reminds us that there is always a bigger picture and brings grace and possibility for harmony in the moment.

Here are two further stories to highlight the triangle of disempowerment and how we jump in thinking we know how to fix something and sometimes make things worse.

It revolves around a small lizard, a pool and me. One day I was checking the skimmer, which picks up leaves, etc. and as I took the lid off a tiny lizard looked up at me from the handle.

"Oh, you don't want to be in there," I said. "Here, let me help you out."

I lifted the cage from the hole, which frightened the lizard, he jumped and fell into the water at which point the suction of the pump pulled him down the hole with the water. I stared in disbelief.

Oh no, I was only trying to help and now he's gone down the pipes and he will be in the filter. I ran down to where the pump was, turned off the pump and took the lid off the filter. I lifted the filter out and as the water drained out there at the bottom was the tiny lizard, alive and looking at me as if to say, "Huh, so you thought you knew what I needed?"

I was so thankful that he was still alive. "I am so sorry," I kept saying. I left the filter on the floor until he made his way out.

Then I got the pool pump working again.

You see, this is just a really simple example. I thought that, one, the lizard was in trouble and then I thought I knew the best thing for him. And it backfired. I was fortunate that I got the lesson and did not harm anything. This is how it happens when we are on the triangle, when we think things need fixing and we think we know how to fix them and then wade in without asking those who we think we are rescuing what they really need or want.

For all I know this tiny lizard may have been in the skimmer because that is where he goes every day for his lunch!

The cashier glares at you as you unload your shopping and reload and pay. It's not personal, you might think it is, but maybe they have had a bad day, they're bored. You really have no idea. Are you going to let them decide how you are going to feel? Here we want to take a breath and hold on to what is true for us. Remember when you left the house you were in a good space? Your day is going okay, maybe it isn't, all the same are you going to let how someone else is behaving influence you?

Once upon a time I was a Mum with young children and I wanted and still do want the best for my kids. My son was an amazing shape shifter when he was a kid. He could imitate most animals and knew everything about them. When he started school he roared at the teacher like a lion when she told him off. She was surprised but this was normal at home. Then like a lot of kids he became interested in dinosaurs and again he would walk like them, sound like them and knew everything there was to know about them. We thought it quite incredible.

Then one day I noticed in the playground he was walking like a dinosaur and the other kids were avoiding him. I thought maybe they think he'll have them for breakfast and again thought nothing of it. Until one day whilst standing with the other Mums I asked them why they were laughing. They explained that they were laughing at my son because he was acting weird. I was mortified. Immediately I decided that I must sort this out. I made an appointment with his teacher about my son's behaviour (which now apparently I had to fix). The teacher thought he was a genius and told me not to worry. Too late, I was, so I booked an appointment with the homoeopath. He came with me because now he got that perhaps there was something wrong with him and he needed fixing.

Well, no matter what I tried nothing changed; in fact it got worse. Then one day at work one of my colleagues said, "Leave him alone!"

"Pardon?" I replied.

She repeated, "Leave him alone, there is nothing wrong with him, you are trying to fix him and he is perfectly okay, it is you that is not ok. Take a look at yourself!"

For a couple of moments I was stunned by this but I got it, she was right, she was like the angel that had shone a light and I could see immediately that this was all my stuff. It was me that had never had many friends and was bullied at school and left out. When I saw the situation with my son, it triggered a memory in my computer files and I went into rescuer mode. Why, because I had projected my victim onto my son and I was doing my best to fix myself through him and he did not need fixing; there was absolutely nothing wrong with him. I had become the perpetrator. I had put us both on the triangle of disempowerment. And it happened without me being aware of it.

I had to let go of my story, look at the shadows and the strategies that I had put in place to survive when I was little. I had to clear up my own back yard. I used the nature painting and another shamanic process to clear the memory from my energy field so that I was no longer available for similar situations to arise. And just three days after I had completed my own personal work, cleared my garden, my son was playing happily with the other kids. Now that was bonkers!

I share this story because I want to emphasize how even with the best intentions we can sometimes cause harm. Of course we want everything to be okay for our kids, for those we love. We do have to be awake though and ask, when we step in to help, from which place are we thinking, feeling and acting. Are we using another to heal our own stuff or to see our own stuff and if so how long are we going to leave that projection out there causing harm to another rather than bringing it back to us. There are many aspects of the shamanic training in this story and in sharing I trust that it will paint a picture which helps us all to see where we interfere in places purely because we are not able to see our own shadow or to accept that we cannot relive our lives through our kids or others or use others to heal our own wounds. We have to take everything back to us and take a good look and change the map of our life. We want to leave the old story behind, acknowledge the shadows and the patterns. See the learning and move on.

When we have the courage to do this we begin to walk lightly on earth leaving no tracks. As we shift our map of life so others have the opportunity to do the same and we do not leave our wounds as a legacy for our children or their children to reconcile.

The shamanic path teaches us that shadow work is the most important personal work we can do and is a continual process. There is never anyone out there to blame, remember everyone you talk about, you're talking about yourself, whether you deem it good or bad. Projections are necessary so that we have the opportunity to see what is going on inside of us. It is how long we leave our projection out there that can disrupt our lives and the lives of others. The quicker we can see and own our shadow, the greater the energy we have to create new coordinates in our map of life. Shadows or unacknowledged parts of ourselves can be driven by a number of things:

Our personal experience from womb to now
Family patterns and beliefs
Society and cultural patterns and beliefs
Our own karmic life experiences (and if past lives are not your thing then the stories that live within you)
The shaman say the greatest gift we can be to the world is to clear up our own yard. If you find yourself thinking you know what needs putting right or fixing out there take a look inside. If you find yourself really reacting to someone else's behaviour, thoughts and emotions look at what it is about that person, what characteristic do you not like or what is it you love about them and then look inside and ask:
Where am I like that?
Could I be like that?
Have I been like that?

And we honour our ancestors and unbind ourselves from the patterns that come down the family line whether these are in the form of emotional or physical patterns.

Chapter 6
North and East

As we step into the North and East directions we become more aware of how quickly we can create exactly what we ask for. We recognize that the inner personal work is essential to maintain a balanced relationship with all aspects of our life. We realize that if we want to dream a world into being we want to create a new version, not a repeat of the old, which is exactly what we will do if we remain closed to the work of the South and West directions of the medicine wheel. In the North and East we begin to step outside of linear time and become more available for synchronistic moments in our lives and life begins to flow.

Intention

Intention is the driving force behind any thought, feeling and action.

With strong intention we can manifest most things. This is the power of our mind and consciousness and our energetic connection to all around us.

Let's face it, anything can become a weapon with the intention to make it so. Any harmful thoughts, words or actions directed at another person with enough heartfelt feeling and intention will hit its target. Thankfully most of the ninety thousand thoughts each one of us has every day pass us by without a second look. This is how we miss our own shadows and beliefs because they just pass by like any habit and we are not even aware of them.

The difference on the other hand is in those thoughts we have, let's say, after a row with our boss or our friend. Two hours after the argument we are still replaying the event in our heads, feeling even more pissed off with him or her. Justifying ourselves and saying all sorts of things internally that perhaps we wanted to but did not have the courage to say to their face. We work ourselves up inside, creating a great surge of energy based on not our feelings but our emotions and together with our thoughts and words this energy goes out to that person. They get it even if you do not encounter them again for several days.

This kind of energetic emission is detrimental both to us and to the person we are directing it towards. Why?

Well, first when you use up your internal energy supply to whiplash someone else you are depleting yourself of vital energy and that heavy energy that you are catapulting through the ether will affect that person's energy field. They may not consciously be aware of your attack but they will feel it on some level.

We all do, you know, expressions like 'I feel like someone has put a knife in my back', 'Stabbed me in the back', 'I feel like I am about to trip up.'

You see the human brain reboots itself roughly every twenty minutes, so if you have an unpleasant encounter, you have feelings about it but you can take a moment to self-enquire, "Why have I been available for this? What is it showing me?" You can take this insight in the moment and move on – great!

Maybe you have an encounter, it is unpleasant but you have no reaction because you have acknowledged your shadow. When you have absorbed shadow you can take yourself much more lightly. A great example of this is when president Lincoln was told by a woman he met on the train that he was one of the ugliest men she'd seen in her entire life. He wasn't offended, he simply asked her, "What should I do about that?" She told him, "You could stay home." This is a story that Lincoln told because he liked the woman's response to his question.

If however two hours, two days or two years down the line we are still having that row, we are still holding a grudge, we have either created an imprint, (a pattern) or activated (an imprint) pattern. Remember those icons on our computer screen, our computer memory banks? Well now they are taking up the whole screen, our whole life.

Long-term situations of this nature only continue to harm all involved, including us. We may think we feel better about blaming and continuing to dish another person, but believe me we are diminishing our own energy reserves, let alone the energy of those around us and that of the person we are in dispute with.

It is so sad because most of the time we are unaware of why we feel so rubbish. All the time we hold blame or unkind thoughts about someone else we affect ourselves. When we send out heavy energy to another we are depleting ourselves. It does affect us. It diminishes us. Every time we are abusive to someone verbally, physically, every time we shout and belittle someone, bully them, we are really diminishing ourselves energetically.

Our mind may rationalize that what we are doing is okay, to get revenge, to attain power or whatever it is we think we need. You see we are trying to fill a space because we feel like something is missing and we may each of us attribute different things here but ultimately it is connection, a feeling that we belong, that we are loved and I mean real love; the energy that is always present, cannot be manipulated, gives nothing and asks for nothing in return. It simply exists.

Every time we attack we affect our own energy, we still have the feeling something is missing. We still feel depleted and so it drives us to do more of the same. We get caught in a vicious circle feeding our need by attacking others and sadly accentuating that need because what we are actually doing is harming ourselves.

We talk about the power of intention all the time in shamanic training. I remember one of the first things that really caught my attention was when my mentor Alberto Villoldo said, "The shaman (that's us by the way) and the sorcerer (and this can be us too) walk the same path; the only difference is that the shaman's intention is to be of service to another and the sorcerer is concerned with gaining personal power."

Let's face it, our identity (EGO) likes to be in charge, it likes to think it is in control, that it has the power to do what it wishes. Most of the time we get upset is when things are not going the way we (our identity/ego) want them to go. Man's greatest fear is the loss of his personal importance. This is simply those moments in everyday life when we throw our toys out of our prams because we are not getting what we think we want. When we take all this into consideration, everything that we have shared together so far, we want to be careful what we ask for. And we want to enquire more regularly what and who is driving this demand.

Our intention is always to be of the highest possible service in any encounter.

The minute we deem anything as needing fixing we are intimating that it is broken, not working, that something is wrong and we know best how to fix it. The universe hears there is something wrong and right now in this moment there is no possibility of fixing this. We want to do our best to see every encounter as an opportunity to make a difference and this involves the participation of everyone. By creating an opportunity the universe hears that right now in this moment it is possible.

We are the ones who can make the difference and we have to start with us. And yes you may have to ask someone to assist and facilitate you on your journey. We are human and we are here to evolve together, we can assist each other. Another can be a silent witness, a guide to assist you so that you can see something that is maybe hidden from your view. Sometimes an intervention can be made on your behalf so that you can create a new map for yourself. The power to shift and transform, to reconcile, always comes from within us, not from outside of us.

The role of a shaman is to be of service to facilitate us on that journey of self-discovery. A shaman never heals you. A shaman knows nothing requires fixing. A shaman knows this encounter is an opportunity for self-enquiry and inner knowledge. A shaman brings you into connection with yourself to find harmony within. The intention is always the outcome that is of the highest possible service. A shaman's role is to assist you to find the key to open the door to your own extraordinary journey.

Projection

We have spoken a lot about shadow, patterns, and roles. Projection is part of our everyday lives and it is useful to know that we are all projecting all the time. The shaman's awareness reminds us that we are all living in a reality that we are creating from within. In quantum physics it has been scientifically proven that energy is benign and responds to the thoughts and expectations of the individuals observing it.

We want to know how to recognize our projections as quickly as possible and it is here where we want to be awake and aware to the words and the thoughts that we have both externally and internally. When we find ourselves in the place of blame or have preconceived ideas how things may be for others without asking them, then there may be a projection worth looking at. I say this because we live most of our lives bobbing along up and down and as things challenge us we often shift anyway without being conscious of the fact. It is when we have an over the top reaction, either outwardly or internally, that we want to take a moment to pause and see what is really going on. When we find ourselves in the same old scenario time and time again whether this is in our health, relationships, work etc. behaving in a way that always makes life uncomfortable or creates a mess. We want to stop and ask ourselves:

Why am I thinking, feeling and behaving in this way?
Call it out from under its rock and see it for what it really is.
When we find ourselves projecting our stuff whether great or not we want to bring the projection back to ourselves, so for example, you may find yourself saying to your partner,
"Why do you never listen to me?"
Stop; ask is this true?

You see you will find that perhaps sometimes your partner does listen.

This is not about your partner, this is about you, and so you have to own the projection. Ask,

Where do I not listen?

Who do I not listen to?

You may find that you don't always listen to people and the person you really don't listen to is yourself. That quiet inner voice of wisdom that you cover over with every kind of external distraction you can in order not to hear.

May be this voice is calling you into shifting your perception of your life and you don't want to because your identity (ego) is scared.

Maybe. So we have to make self-enquiry. And it is here that we usually come across what we call back doors.

This is a term used for all the reasons why not? All those reasons it is not possible to shift or change something or stay for that matter in our new map, our new version of our life.

Back doors are great; they keep us stuck where we do not want to be (or do we) or even if we do shift, a part of our energy is constantly draining away and maintaining that back door for us.

Here are a few back doors that have raised their heads in my own life and in classes I have facilitated.

I can't move forward until I figure it out

I have too many negative thoughts; I cannot be a shaman

I don't have enough experience

I'll never be as good as

When I get my certificate then

I'm not ready yet

There's plenty of time what's the hurry?

If this doesn't work then I'll just go back

I'm too old to do this

I'm too young to do this

There's never enough time

I need more time

When I get my office decorated

The kids are too young

I'll be qualified enough after the next course, the next and the next.

The dog ate my notes

If I put myself out there then I have to take myself seriously

I'm just not fully available right now

Each of these reasons for not stepping up for our lives is driven by something or someone. We have to have the bigger picture, the whole vision because in all of our journeys we have to be guided by where we are in our lives. We have to make realistic decisions and yet there are moments when we can follow our intuition, when we may make what seem like unrealistic decisions to some but create a great opportunity where we take ourselves outside of our comfort zone.

Yes, sometimes it is wise to have an exit strategy. This is a conscious plan and we want to be fully aware of how much of our energy we put there. If we are working and constantly thinking about a way out, we cannot be present to what we are doing or where we are; our energy is someplace else.

We want to be as present and centred in ourselves as possible to ask clear questions about the direction of our life's path and receive the messages from the encounters we have so we are always evolving and participating in our journey.

A Story of Projection

So here is a client's experience. I have not given any names to protect the confidentiality between us but I am very grateful to her for allowing me to use this story to highlight the awareness necessary when we embark on the shamanic path.

It was Saturday morning and I was acutely aware that in our conversations my husband was emphasizing the fact that I had not done much. Everything he asked me concerning little things being finished or done my answer was no. This had happened before and I had ignored it, thinking that I did not want to engage with this conversation. But of course I was engaged because inside I was becoming more and more pissed off. With thoughts like 'he thinks I do nothing', 'nobody appreciates me or what I do'.

Sound familiar to anyone. Well this was shadow working out!

So I continued my silence and made breakfast, I was asked if I had put the coffee machine on to which I replied, no. He made some comment under his breath, kind of joking but I did not take it that way. Then he asked if his breakfast was ready. I was infuriated inside but said nothing apart from "I am doing it now."

He joked, "I suppose I'll have to do it just like everything else"

By this time I was getting really angry inside, fully engaged but thinking I won't engage I'm just going to ignore him. I asked him if he wanted jam or marmalade; he asked for jam and as I put the jam on the bread he told me that it was just like the breakfast he has at work. I replied, "I bet you don't get as much jam as I have given you." He replied, "I get more actually, it is usually dripping with jam."

"Why are you always criticizing me? Why is nothing I ever do good enough?" I cried. He replied to me, "I didn't, I just answered your question." He was right, he had purely answered the question I had asked him. I turned to myself and said, "Well you set yourself up for that one." I smiled and I asked myself why I had seen it that way.

I could feel the anger and frustration in my belly. What is my story here?

Nothing I ever do is good enough. I used my shamanic tools to release some of the heavy energy around my belly. I did not need the story, I could feel it.

I decided to take it to an image of a river and returning to the source of my river I found a tiny stick. I was surprised it was so small because it felt huge. I breathed the energy out to release the image of this small stick and followed the river. I saw a dam, which would have held the water back but for one small gap where this small stick had once been.

Slowly but surely I saw the force of the river weaken and push the dam of sticks away. By moving the small stick I had weakened the dam and suddenly my river was flowing again. I could feel this inside.

You see, you don't have to go back and know all the story, if you do you may hang onto it – it's human nature. Using the image of the river my client did not need the detail; she knew the stick represented those internal feelings and beliefs and by releasing it through imagery she was working energetically much quicker than talking it through internally, which would have probably served to make her more emotional and likely to hang on to her story, shadow, emotions and behaviours.

I asked myself simply what did I want instead and I got the image of the river moving with purpose and I could feel this purpose inside. The words were, everything I do has purpose, I am enough.

Now I know that I had to anchor this into everyday life. So every time I make breakfast I focus on how the preparation of breakfast is of service and provides for my family. I am enough is what I finally got. This whole experience lasted forty minutes. I had been playing out this pattern with its beliefs and actions a long time. The difference was in that moment I was awake enough to see myself truly. I have covered this pattern in all sorts of disguises but can see that my life has been about me proving my belief and that I was not enough and that nothing I ever did was enough. My first thoughts had been say nothing, do not engage, he's just playing games (another projection). No, I was the one playing games with myself. Non-engagement in this instant was a strategy to stop myself from seeing myself.

Non-engagement is not about not interacting, it is being fully aware of the situation and remaining balanced in thoughts, feelings and actions so that we respond from a different level of engagement and in service.

I am so grateful for the wisdom I have gained through working with these shamanic tools and how easy it is to shift things when you can be awake enough to see yourself and choose to shift the level at which you respond. I realize I could have made my husband wrong and we could have spent the rest of the day in the silence of discomfort, and I could have kept my belief about myself, continued with the same behaviours, attracting similar situations, but I was able to see myself and choose to create a difference in the moment. It is really magic when we learn to use this wisdom in this way.

So there was a projection:

Why are YOU criticizing? You indicated the projection.

Who was actually criticizing? My client but she may not have accepted this. The person she criticized the most was herself and yet she saw that she did criticize others, just not to their faces, and this was not very comfortable for her to see. She had to own the projection and you can hear in my client's language that "to criticize" and "nothing is ever good enough" go hand in hand.

So by criticizing herself, she could never be good enough.

Good enough for what? There was no definition, so as I know from experience this can play out in all areas, family, work, friends, sport, dancing, the list goes on and on. Where in her life did she decide that this was a good strategy? Something happened sometime, somewhere, and this protected someone or her, or got someone or her through a situation. So was it hers or did she inherit this set of beliefs, feelings and behaviours? And what were they protecting her from?

This is where it gets tricky when we are on our own because our identity is very clever and will convince us in no uncertain terms that the behaviour is justified. We can talk ourselves around and around until we just think, oh well, at least I've seen it. Here is where we want to step into the level of engagement on a more energetic level and we use imagery, looking at where this pattern originated. We can use our life as a river. We set the intention that we want to see the source of the pattern, the shadow, and the belief. As Shaman we always want the origin not the five hundredth version of the same story. We want the very origin from which everything else came.

At the source of her river she found a tiny stick, which surprised her because it felt huge (remember when we have things hidden in our bags, they can seem huge but when the light shines on them we realize that actually they aren't as big as we had imagined, maybe uncomfortable but manageable.) And when she released this energy through using her breath and made her way back down her river she saw a dam, which was complete, and big enough to hold the whole river back, except for one small spot where a tiny stick had once been. And now that stick was no longer in place the force of the river finding a way through this tiny gap was enough to push the whole dam out of the way so that the river flowed freely.

She could really feel this shift inside and I could ask what this shift was, this feeling, this different vibration that she was now aware of. "I am enough," she replied. That's it, no bells and whistles but a huge piece for her personally.

Seeing it is the key, yes, but you have to take the next step otherwise you just keep playing the same record over and over. So this was her game, you see it was easier to blame others for criticizing her, that way she could justify not bothering, not going full steam ahead with her dreams, with her plans. She was protecting herself from something, failure or humiliation, we cannot know, and the detail is not important here, but she did create this strategy because of an experience somewhere, sometime or perhaps she inherited this pattern and just kept playing it out. It matters not, it matters that she was awake enough to see it and after forty-six years she was finally able to recognize herself in this way. Acknowledge this pattern, this old friend (remember her identity saw this as an old friend). We are so clever at disguising the parts of ourselves together with the behaviours that our identity truly believes are protecting us. This is why honouring the old ways of being are so important. You know that the more we try to get rid of something the more tightly it will hang on. It will cling to us like a limpet, changing its appearance and becoming more and more clever at its disguise. The answer is in the word try. Try is about having a go and can have a huge number of exit strategies and reasons why not, depending on what patterns, beliefs you have running on your computer screen.

In honouring the pattern, shadow, belief and all that was involved she was saying thank you, as if she was thanking a loyal friend who had been with her for years.

Thanks for supporting me to this point in my life and for teaching me. This way the pattern feels it has been of service and still is now in a much more positive way for what you have is the learning, the nugget of gold from all the experiences and this is all you have to take with you, nothing else. And if the old behaviour should come knocking my client can use it as a red flag to remind her that she now lives in a different house and that her experience of herself in her life is now very different. So you can open the door, say hi to the old way of being and say thank you for reminding me that I live here now, I feel, think and act differently. Thank you again. Then you shut the door, you do not invite the old friend in to take a seat on your sofa. By thanking it for reminding you, you create a place where this part feels it is still of service and therefore there is no conflict created.

When we release from an energetic level our vibration shifts, we are no longer available for situations or encounters that keep emphasizing the old pattern. We have the gift and our vibration has shifted. My client's self-awareness opened up and a thread of consciousness occurred and in that moment she saw the learning and the nugget of gold was seen.

My client shared shortly after this work that from the moment she got it, her husband's behaviour shifted. He no longer had to become the actor in her play.

And life shifted not just at home but in all areas of her life. She shared, *"My experience of life is new and it is great and it is magic!"*

As we journey through life we are constantly moving around the medicine wheel. If you like, the medicine wheel becomes a map that assists us in every moment because it follows the circle; there is no beginning or end. There is no past or future; only now. The wheel teaches us to walk lightly on the earth to release ourselves from our stories, it teaches us to walk as the luminous warrior with no enemies in this world or the next, it teaches us to live consequently, we realize there are ripples that go out as a result of our thoughts, feelings and actions. And it teaches us how to transcend or to go beyond a certain belief, a pattern, an old outmoded behaviour, and how to create new coordinates in our map of life. This in turn opens the door for a new way of thinking, feeling and behaving.

Now this doesn't mean that you find yourself in a new job or a new relationship. You may still be doing the same job, you are still in the same relationship; the difference is within you. You meet your job, your relationship from a new place. And from this new place that you have created others have the opportunity to shift too and so creating an opportunity for new possibilities.

Of course sometimes we may encounter people or situations that are incredibly stubborn in their persistence to stay exactly as they are. And we can do nothing about this. We cannot make others change. We can still make the shift within us and at this point there is a place where we can choose or see a path that calls us. This is where we may change our jobs, our relationships, we may choose to turn the other cheek, we may decide to no longer keep the company of certain people. Remember though as shaman we do not blame or harm anything or anyone with intention. As we shift our vibration, our lives, our awareness heightens and we can be more available for the opportunities as they present themselves. Here is where we can take that pause to listen to the quiet internal voice. It has a persistent tone but it never demands that you act immediately.

We want to be in alignment, right thought, right feelings and right actions. We want to be willing to listen to our quiet voice and bring our inner voice into right relationship with the voice of our identity (ego), so that the wisdom of the two helps us to seek a higher outcome for all involved.

And yes, sometimes it is uncomfortable. And sometimes we do not want to take the opportunity. This is okay too, for we know that the encounters will keep occurring until we do, and if we keep refusing to take the opportunity the encounters will get more and more intense, bigger and bigger until we take the learning and move on.

An Example of Resistance to Change and Synchronicity

When my husband mentioned over six years ago that he had seen a job he really wanted and it was in France, I knew the job was his. I do not know how I knew, I just had a feeling. We had a conversation about what it would mean if he got the job and I said that we would deal with those things as and when they were necessary.

So after numerous interviews, guess what, he got the job.

Then the reality hit home. First we made arrangements for my husband to rent in France and come home to England each weekend. We began this new routine; it wasn't easy for any of us. But I most certainly did not want to leave my family and friends. Then my youngest son fractured his wrist and shortly after he had recovered my oldest son injured his wrist on the same side. He had twisted it so badly the doctor said it would have been better if he had broken it.

This time I stopped and thought, both wrists same side – indicating a split, the family was split. But the thought of going to live in France, giving up my work, scared me, so we just carried on. I was tired, my husband was tired. I take my hat off to single parents. I then taught a class with Alberto and whilst doing a shadow exercise with Alberto he shared with me an image of a woman crying and the sense was she knew she was never going back. I had a feeling I knew what it was about, but I was not about to acknowledge it because I didn't want to.

Got home, back into the routine, work, kids, home and all the things that involves.

Then one day I had to go into town, only for twenty minutes. I parked the car really easily. There was nobody around and just a few cars in the car park. I went to the post office, came back and immediately knew something was not right. I looked at the car and there was a note on the windscreen; it read, 'I am so sorry, I hit your car whilst parking.'

I looked up, the car park was empty but this person had chosen to park right next to me and hit the car. No way! Oh yes, and the front of the car was damaged. They had made a good job of it; two thousand pounds' worth!

In this instant I got it.

"Okay, I am not supposed to be here, in the UK, I get it, I am going to France. I get it, you hear, I don't need any more signs." Thank you. And thank you for the note.

I really did not want any more signs from the universe, this was enough, I know that they would have got bigger if I had continued to resist.

So arrangements were made and we moved to France. How stubborn was I?

To mark this in a shamanic way, I created a small parcel with a photo of us as a family with some sugar, rice and flowers to say thank you to our home and the land we had lived upon, to say thanks and goodbye.

Then in France I created another parcel to say thank you to the land we live on and our new home. A simple action but thank you goes a long way and during the moments when I buried these parcels in the earth I knew that France was where I was meant to be and where I currently am. My learning was to acknowledge that we never go back. Going back is in the past and as such is done. Going back to a place can never be the same or replicated. Even if the experience is similar it is never the same. We get disappointment when we have expectations, most of which are based on something we experienced once upon a time in the past.

So now I live in France, I have had to go beyond my story that I am an English woman living in France. Now I am a woman living in France. My kids are bilingual, my husband almost and me? Well that's another story I am working with!

Synchronistic Moments

We are all aware of synchronistic moments; you know when you think of someone and the phone goes and it is them. You are in a shop looking for a book and one falls off the shelf or looks brighter than the others. And remarkably it is the one you are looking for. The more awake and aware we are the more available we are for these moments, these encounters and the messages they are bringing us.

The Cucumber Story

Once upon a time I had a client who lived close by so I agreed to go to her house for the session we had arranged.

During the session I got the image of a cucumber and because of the kind of session we were doing this was a gift. For a while I argued that there must be something else because I (the performer) was worried about what my client might think when I gave her a cucumber as a gift. You see, for a moment here I was not in service of another, I was more concerned with how I may look; stupid, don't know what I am doing, etc. Eventually I managed to get over myself, accept that this was the gift and took a huge breath as I explained to my client what the gift was. She was delighted with her cucumber; she knew exactly what this gift was showing her. It was a medicinal gift for her.

I learned that when I am the performer I am only concerned with self-preservation, and with maintaining the known and safe identity. I trust my intuition and know that being true is more of service to another than self-preservation. The funny thing was, that after I left my client's house I crossed over the road. As I did so I saw something in the middle of the pavement. As I got closer, I saw it was a cucumber! I looked up and down the road, expecting to see someone with a shopping bag or someone unloading his or her car. Not a person was seen. There was nothing in the street except the cucumber and me. Anyone looking out of his or her window may have considered I had lost the plot, as I was walking around the cucumber looking up at the sky and back to the cucumber. It was as if it had fallen out of the sky. Again, I got it, really! The gift was a cucumber. Thank you! I am really grateful that I did not argue about something bigger like a lion or an elephant. I chuckled to myself all the way home – bloomin' bonkers!

So we are of service in our daily lives when we are not thinking of ourselves as the performer. We are always looking for the highest wisdom in the face of the person we are with and hold a place for the highest outcome to be possible. And this we can do at home, at work, in the supermarket, in confrontation, in all areas of our lives. Yes, it takes awareness, it takes practice and it is necessary to remember the tools we have that can help us.

The Fly Story

Once upon a time during a vision quest a participant created her vision quest circle in a beautiful spot. As is the custom, from the moment we arrive the only words spoken are by the facilitator. This was an eight hour vision quest and the preparations had gone well. I set up my base so that everyone knew where I was and with the sound of the drum everyone left for his or her quest.

Eight hours later I began to drum everyone back. Slowly, very slowly, everyone returned to the meeting point. One of the participants had left her bag whilst she had gone to retrieve something from her space. You could not help but notice that her bag was covered in flies and I mean covered in them. The flies did not move onto any other bag or person, just this one bag belonging to this lady.

No words were spoken until we had returned to the retreat and participated in the welcoming home ceremony. Then, all sitting in a circle, the talking stick was placed in the middle of the circle and when each person was ready to share they picked up the talking stick and said their first words. This is often a very moving moment.

The participant with the bag covered in flies picked up the talking stick and began to recount how, after having chosen a beautiful spot, she settled down in her vision quest circle to go to sleep. As soon as she lay down all these flies turned up and they would not leave her alone. She explained how she had no food or anything with her that she knew would attract flies; she checked the area she was questing on to ensure she had not created her circle on a pile of poo, she even left her circle to hang from the branch of a nearby tree to get rid of the flies, but they followed her everywhere. She explained how she was so desperate to go to sleep but the flies would not let her sleep.

What this had shown her was that she used sleep as a strategy to step out of life. She explained how she had come to the vision quest thinking it was a place to escape her life. On the contrary the vision quest, like all ancient teachings, is about becoming more conscious, more awake and more aware.

She had certainly stayed awake with the help of those flies and had taken the opportunity to see herself and recognize the wisdom in the experience. This was an incredible learning not just for this extraordinary woman but also for the whole group.

Finding a Place Story

During pipe ceremony there was a young man who appeared unsettled.

During pipe ceremony, like vision quest you find what we call a sit spot, a place you can go to, to be quiet and reflect within as the class progresses. Right from the beginning this young man was unable to find a spot; a place that he wanted to settle in. He came to me for help.

His story so far for his life had been about creating some coordinates for himself to create a place for himself in the world.

I acknowledged this was a challenge and invited him to take the opportunity to create a place for himself, his own space during this class, regardless of how uncomfortable this was. I did not tell him where to create the space or how, I just invited him to take the opportunity that was presenting itself.

Without saying any more, I noticed that he had in fact created a sit spot, but what he had done was created a circle just like a vision quest and he was sitting in the centre of his circle. Eighteen months later I learned that he had a job and a place to live that he had chosen. And he did it; he created it. These tools, these teachings are about empowering each and every one of us to evolve within our own life journey, within the evolution of our families, societies and cultures.

What I took from this experience was how it is so important for teenagers to begin to create their own coordinates, guided, yes, with some kind of rite of passage that acknowledges that they are moving from the realm of a child into the realm of adulthood. Without this rite of passage or acknowledgement they can become lost in the matrix of the world and be vulnerable to false promises of acknowledgement. Boundaries are necessary, they are like the coordinates that we work within and shift and change as we take our adventure of life. We have to have coordinates so that we know where we are. Then when we want to change direction we can imagine or know where we want our new coordinates to be.

I have experienced truly that when we make an effort, when we meet people halfway, then there is an opportunity, a possibility.

Moving to France

When I first moved to France, I did not say much or try to interact, largely because I did not speak French and I realized that I was embarrassed. I took myself far too seriously. I remembered people telling me how arrogant the French are. Well, for the record, that is a projection, we all have the characteristic of arrogance within us. Take us English, we expect others to speak English and understand us, often without making the effort to learn the native language.

My experience has been of beautiful people, willing to help, willing to share and willing to accept us as a family into their friendship. Yes there have been encounters that have not been so great but these encounters happened for a reason. They revealed something to us about ourselves. By not revealing ourselves opportunity and possibility could not evolve.

We already know how powerful our beliefs, thoughts, feelings and actions are and how they can influence what and how we experience our life. We begin to learn that by raising our vibration, just in the way that we engage with the world can make a huge difference. We also begin to realize, when we can stay awake long enough, how important it is to keep a check on what we are truly asking the universe for, by way of our patterns beliefs, thoughts, feelings and actions, because we begin to experience the speed at which we can manifest these things.

Like you want to envision a new career, fulfilling and using your skills beyond what you know. Remember though, if you still have a pattern hanging around, or a belief that it won't work or that it won't happen or that the other person is better than you, or that the boss is a jerk. Believe me, you will get more of that rather than what you envision and you will get it more quickly until that is you can shift the vibration that continues to attract these things to you.

Being in alignment is being aware that what you present on the outside has to be the same as you on the inside. The more we acknowledge all of us we become more condensed and full up on the inside. Then it is no longer necessary to go into battle to win and take energy from others (in whatever form we choose).

The challenge for all of us is to know that the highest possible vibration, outcome, is always available to us. It is only our fears and patterns, etc. that stop us from achieving this.

Where terrible things have happened it is incredibly challenging to manage our emotions towards those who have been a part of those situations. We cannot condone awful acts; there is a moral intelligence and the sacredness of all of life as a reference point that most of us come back to. We know from this work, however, that by harbouring resentment, hatred and all those emotions we experience, it makes it less likely for reconciliation to occur in this generation or the next. And this does affect us all on a personal level and on the global level because we are mirrors of each other. It is sad that most reconciliation is done on our deathbeds or as we die – maybe this is because in the moment of death we finally wake up to what our purpose was. What we had foreseen we would do when we were born but for reasons we cannot always explain, we didn't manage to fulfil what we set out to do.

The experiences and influences in our early years can create a map that fuels a need for energy and power that we rationalize is okay because it is the only way that we know how to survive or to get what we think we want. Maybe we are searching for revenge and power or love and understanding. And somehow our mind, complex as it is, convinces us that it is okay to do awful things to each other. Maybe we become the target of many people's shadow and so just as with the triangle of disempowerment it is very challenging to get out of this role. We have to look at why we are available to take on such a huge role for so many people but how we manage this can also create the opportunity for others to wake up to the fact that they are projecting their own shadows out into the world. We talk about creating heaven on earth. Heaven is here, we just haven't woken up and seen it yet.

Chapter 7

Death

Death plays a huge part in the training of the shaman; not literally but symbolically. Here are some of the thoughts around death and a brief guide to the natural process itself, a verse from an old manuscript submitted by a member of the Grace family, Ruth Burton, Nanaimo, British Columbia.

Out of This World...

Out of this world I shall never take
Things of silver and gold I make.
All that I cherish and hoard away
After I leave this world must stay.
Tho I have toiled for a painting rare
To hang on the wall I must leave it there,
Tho I call it mine and boast its worth
I must give it up when I leave this earth.
All that I gather and all that I keep
I must leave it behind when I fall asleep.
And I often wonder what I shall own
In that other life when I pass alone.
What shall they find and what shall they see
In the soul that answers the call for me?
Will the great judge learn when my talk is thru
That my spirit has gathered some riches too?

Here, at this place, is a moment to bring death out from its hiding place.

We don't really like to talk about death in the West, although we are getting better at it. There are two sure things in life once we have been born. At some point we will pay tax and we will at some point die.

There is a coffin out there for every one of us and it is part of the cycle of life and death. This cycle is occurring within us and around us all the time; in our natural surroundings, within us, both on a cellular, physical and emotional level, every day of our lives. Our cells die and rejuvenate constantly, death occurs in order that new life can be realized. Equally throughout our lives we are dying to one stage of our lives in order to step into the next. You die to an old way of working to begin a new role. A child leaving home for the first time to start school dies to being an infant and lives into the first steps of independence. The child turning in to the teenager dies to the child and begins the journey into adulthood.

Sometimes we have to die to a friendship the way it was. Sometimes we may return to that friendship meeting at a different level or maybe it was a friendship for that part of our journey and we must die to the relationship to move on.

We die to many encounters almost every day where there is an opportunity to learn more about ourselves. And maybe similar encounters continue to show up until we finally see the message for us. We look inward, to an old belief, an old feeling and old behaviour. Our vibration shifts and we step into a new way of being. So we experience many symbolic deaths in our journey through life and these are essential if we want to participate in living fully.

As I have mentioned previously, what we fear will find us. If death is feared it will continue to stalk us. We find ourselves always looking over our shoulders waiting for death to show up, or in our fear of death we become dead inside, we appear to be alive but we are not living, we are just going through the motions of being alive. I know what I prefer, even if I do get blisters!

A Short Story

A certain merchant in Baghdad sent his servant to the market to buy some provisions. A little while later, the servant returned, looking white in the face. In a trembling voice he said, "Just now in the market place I was jostled by a man in the crowd, and when I turned I saw it was Mr Death. He looked at me and made a threatening gesture. Please lend me your horse, because I want to go to Samara where Mr Death will not be able to find me."

The merchant agreed and lent the scared man his horse. The servant mounted the horse and rode away as fast as the animal could gallop. Later that day, the merchant went down to the market place and saw Mr Death standing in the crowd. He approached him and said, "Why did you make a threatening gesture to my servant when you saw him this morning?"

"That was not a threatening gesture," said Mr Death. "It was only a start of surprise. I was astonished to see him in Baghdad, because I have an appointment with him tonight in Samara."

Here is another wonderful piece by Robert Fulghum.

"Between the first inhale at birth and the last exhale at death are all the little deaths and revivals. Some part of us is always dying..."

When I graduated from school and left home, a world died. Most of the people I had seen every day, I never saw again as surely as if they were dead. And the same thing happened when I changed jobs, moved to a new city, or from one part of town to another. Those who leave their native land to take up a new life in a new country know about this. As do those who get divorced.

When we've changed our religious views or political convictions, a part of our past dies. When love ends; be it the first mad romance of adolescence, the love that will not sustain a marriage, or the love of a failed friendship, it is the same. A death.

Likewise in the event of a miscarriage or an abortion, the possibility is dead. And there is no public or even private funeral. Sometimes only regret and nostalgia mark the passage. And the last rites are held in solitude of one's most secret self – a service of mourning in the tabernacle of the soul.

Crossing these thresholds is a rite of passage. Revival is a lifelong ritual. Nothing amazes me about being human more than this capacity for revival.

The ritual of revival has many names; 'born again' or 'the urge to reassemble the fragments of our lives into a whole is powerful'.

Death first... then life!

So every time we shift our level of engagement, acknowledge and reconcile our shadows, honour our past, our stories, our genetic and karmic stories, we are honouring the role death plays symbolically in order that we truly participate fully in living. This way death becomes an ally, reminding us to live as fully as we can in every moment.

We sometimes hear stories from soldiers who, despite the adversity, thrive on the constant tightrope wire of life and death. Almost the sense of possible death brings with it the fullness of living or being alive. Shaman know that we do not need to be at war to experience living fully, that our relationship with death and its symbol assists us to wake up and live more consciously. Despite the challenge this is attainable in any moment. It means we begin to become more flexible. That movement in our journey of life is more graceful.

Death – The Natural Process

As a result of technology, more 'near death' experiences have been recorded than ever before and the sharing always includes some kind of life review. My sense is that we get to watch our life as if it was a movie and see the moments when maybe we did make a difference and those moments when we missed an opportunity. At death my sense is we have to face ourselves. Not another but ourselves; we are our own judge. Whatever our religion or faith, my sense is that somewhere in all scriptures there is a cord or unity urging us to recognize the highest wisdom and purpose of all humankind for humankind. Now I totally get that on an individual level when we look out at the world we can say,

"What difference can I make?"

All the difference in the world, is what I say. Our ancestors like us had to evolve, they had to endure, they had to learn, yes they had to fight and have courage.

We want the courage to bring our families, societies, our cultures and ourselves into a place of unity, recognizing the significant influence each one of us has on the bigger picture. The reconciliation personally will influence those around us and, just like the one cell of the caterpillar that informs all the other cells how to transform into a butterfly, we can do the same.

So I have touched on death earlier and here I would like to share some thoughts on death and the process. We are all going to die but how and when, well that remains a mystery to us. And we do not want to spend our life looking over our shoulder waiting for death to turn up like the servant in Bagdad. If we are always looking over our shoulder for death then we cannot be fully alive and living. We want to be in right relationship with death so that we are present to our life in every moment, living our life to the full.

Sometimes we can be alive but dead inside; this is not what death wants. Death is here to help us die to the old in order that we can continue to renew on all levels. That is until our transitional crossing, our final rite of passage.

We want to honour death, to acknowledge that it is inevitable. A right relationship with death helps us to die to those old patterns, beliefs, feelings and actions so that we can be present for the highest possible outcome in our life's journey.

There are a number of ideas about what happens when we die. Personally I like to see it as a bridge, a way to cross from this part of our journey to the next. Perhaps the only way we ever know is when we finally take that final crossing from this lifetime.

Shaman say the journey of life is to grow rainbow bodies (that is to release all our heavy energy in way of patterns, beliefs, all our old computer icons) so that our energy is light and unencumbered. This way legend and lore says that as we depart our energy field collapses, our chakras disengage from the physical body and our energy field passes through our seventh chakra, which is the size of a molecule. Can you imagine getting your entire luggage through that hole? Oh my God! Could be a bit of a struggle.

If we have too much to carry and cannot pass over fully then maybe we get stuck in a lower place to do our reconciliation there. I know what I would rather do and from experience I recognize how valuable it is to have a human body in order that we can accomplish this inner journey to create a rainbow body, which enables us to die consciously

There is a flow to the behaviours and events that occur as we begin to prepare ourselves for this journey. I know that being aware of these, together with the shamanic teachings I choose, held me strong during my mum's final weeks before she died. Knowing how the physical body reacts and having a sense of the dying person's process really helped me to be of service to my mum rather than becoming absorbed in my own drama around my mum's death.

It is so important to remember everyone else involved and to honour the fact that each one of us deals with the death of someone in our own way. It is really our own way of coming to terms with our own mortality. We can offer a hand, we can invite people to look at ways of coping, but everyone has their own relationship with death and every one of us has a different relationship with the person who has died or is dying. There are many ways we choose to honour our loved ones and it is up to us to discover the way which is most of service to our grieving process and the passing of the person. For example, when my mum passed away, I created a small altar in the garden with a pot of flowers, which has since become my ancestor altar. My dad puts out a candle every night without fail. We all have to find our own way.

In sudden death, the processes are the same, they happen instantaneously and even sometimes on reflection those close to the person remember changes in behaviour that now make sense. As if the person who has departed had some sense, conscious or unconscious, that they were not staying with us very long.

The shamanic teachings I talk of brought me to a place where I did not feel like I lost my mum and to this day I know she is not lost. I touched something that confirmed this when my mum finally passed away and to this day I still cannot find a word that would describe the experience. I wish I could.

Dying is a natural process and the more familiar we become with what this process is the less fear we have, the less we feel like something is wrong and that it is down to us to fix it. My mum was diagnosed with cancer shortly after I moved to France. The toughest part was the not knowing what that really meant, whether Mum would recover, whether she would suffer. It is the suffering of another that is the hardest to witness.

When disease arrives in the body it is a messenger; we ask how can I respond to what has come into my life, as opposed to believing we are responsible for the illness, which can lead to feelings of guilt and the necessity to fight. We do not want to make our illness an enemy; the illness is a part of us. I felt helpless, I wanted to fix it for my mum, but that was something I knew I could not do. Why; because there is never anything to fix, only an opportunity to evolve, an opportunity to reconcile. I could have worked energetically with my mum but without her consent this would have been for my sake and not hers.

My mum took her own journey with her cancer. Yes, we talked, but she didn't like to speak about it too much because she felt like that would give too much energy to the cancer. So that's how it was.

When we begin to prepare to die, the body naturally withdraws and we begin to lose our appetite so we begin to eat less food; this is the body's way of sustaining life. We begin to switch from a physical energy source to a more energetic source and we experience weight loss.

The body is preserving itself and, as digestion takes such a lot of energy, it is wise for the digestive system to slow down so that the body can conserve energy for the other more important functions, like those of the heart and lungs.

As those around the dying person we may think they're starving to death and feel that they should eat more. Some people who are dying will force themselves to eat to keep those around them happy whilst experiencing much discomfort themselves. The best we can do is to listen to the requests of the dying person, allow them to say how and what and when they want things.

My mum was clear about this and at each meal time my dad would ask my mum what she wanted and sometimes her plate would consist of 1 potato, 1 brussel sprout and a slice of meat.

The heavier foods were the first to disappear, like meat and cheese, and slowly through Mum's process we came to a point where she would only take those meal replacement drinks. I realized that whilst we were concerned that Mum might be hungry or thirsty her natural withdrawal actually helped keep her as comfortable as she could be. If we had demanded feeding tubes or IVs during the last weeks of Mum's life, it would have served only us and made her uncomfortable. Why; because the body has an innate wisdom which overrides ours and if we had put an IV in place the body was in no position to utilize it so we could have created problems like oedema and swelling, making Mum uncomfortable and causing her distress.

We spent time instead reading her stories, talking and remembering old times. Towards the end she had little energy even for that and I learned how we nourish a person by purely being present with them. When Mum knew no more could be done, she seemed to acknowledge that it was her time to go.

Going Inside

Throughout Mum's process it was evident that she began to turn inwards. In the beginning she reduced the trips she made out of the house and the people she interacted with. She stopped her out in the world activities mainly because she did not have the energy to do so.

Turning inwards is a deeply personal process and when we become reflective about our life. Some people talk openly about events that happened, not necessarily in the order that they occurred, but as they show up from memory. Like a life review where we ask things like, what has my life meant?

Is there anything left unfinished?

We begin to look at circumstances, relationships and how we would have preferred things to be. Time becomes very precious indeed. And it may be that this stays completely internal and as family and friends we have to respect the choice of the dying person. I remember with Mum we looked at family photos, recounted stories of how we remembered events. We laughed, we cried and we shared. Gradually Mum would sleep more frequently and this then became longer and the times when Mum was awake were more precious, although I didn't always realize it at the time.

The sleeping is necessary; a lot of internal work is going on – the dying person's consciousness is expanding and dreams and insights can occur that support the process. There can be an awareness of 'the other side'.

And with Mum it was as though she had gone somewhere and then returned; it was a strange time but most certainly there were altered states of awareness.

Symptom and Pain Control

We want the dying person to be comfortable so that the quality of the life they have left is the best it can be.

The hospice nurses were fantastic and Mum received all the help she needed medically. And this meant that she could stay at home, which was her greatest wish.

The doctors and nurses know what can bring the most effective relief to pain so it is with great humility that I thank all those involved in keeping Mum comfortable. Including my dad, whose dedication and love to Mum was beautiful to witness.

Fear of Dying

I asked Mum if she was scared. She responded, "Yes a little, because you don't know what's going to happen."

It is the process of dying that often scares us, not death itself. In the last few weeks Mum seemed more peaceful within, as though she had surrendered to the process, like she had let go of the need to hang on here. Her relationship with dying was incredible to witness, truly graceful.

There were numerous occasions when Mum would look like she was ready to leave, only to come back in a huge burst of energy. I remember one time we had been advised by the hospice nurse that it was possible Mum may go. We all prepared ourselves; I remember I felt low and heavy. Nobody felt like cooking, so I said I'd go and get some fish and chips. A couple of my close friends had been round to see Mum and they had been able to have a chat and a laugh about old times when we were all young! They took me to get the fish and chips; I had no idea if Mum would still be there when I got home. Well I arrived home, my brother answered the door saying, "You'll never guess what!"

"What?"

"Mum has just asked for a gin and tonic!"

What a roller coaster; we had all prepared ourselves for Mum's departure and instead she had ordered a gin and tonic! How amazing, we smiled and laughed, what else were we going to do? And yes, Mum had her gin and tonic and enjoyed it.

Visions

Often people, as they withdraw from eating and drinking, go into natural fasting states. They can report experiences of seeing loved ones who have gone before them and usually have a reassuring sense about them when the dying person recounts their experience. Mum knew her Mum was there but she was waiting for her Dad. Visions are reassuring to the dying person and we can talk to the dying person about who they are seeing, using questions like:

Do you know the people?
Tell me about whom you are seeing.
Are they reassuring or do they upset you?
You can relax, they are there and they're there for you.

These experiences are common and when the dying and those around them accept this is okay then it makes the situation comfortable for the dying person. Negating what they are seeing can be very distressing for the dying person. Visions are considered a part of the process.

Hallucinations can happen if there is disease and overwhelming toxicity in the brain and sometimes in liver disease. There is a difference between visions and hallucinations. With hallucinations the person can appear confused, distressed, agitated, and perhaps saying that they want to go home, to leave the place they find themselves. What they are seeing is not a comfort to them.

If they have been visioning and the person who cares for them is open to this, then this can be an aide to the person. During the process of dying we still make sense of our communication, in that conversations can be appropriate and logical. They are not confused in any way and the person is very aware that what they are experiencing is different to normal life, as they have known it.

When there is nonsensical speech or the person is restless, this could be an indication of hallucination. We can ask in these moments if there is anyone there who can help them or, if we are aware of their visions and reassuring experiences, maybe we can use these to help them in times of distress.

So these stages are known to those involved in assisting the dying person as the pregnancy of the dying process. The withdrawal from fluids, food and visioning is the beginning.

The middle phase is when we begin to notice a change in the person's breath – it becomes irregular. We may be witness to breath, breath, breath – pause.

Now this pause can last between a few seconds to over a minute and then the person will begin to breathe again. The medical term is apnoea – meaning without breath. And it can be very distressing for those caring for the dying person, as it seems like this is perhaps the final breath. This is normal in the process and can last a few hours to a few days. This passes and the transition stage follows.

During the transition phase the person can become restless and may moan and look uncomfortable. This is like when a baby is born, the transition phase just before the baby is born can be the most uncomfortable when we do not know where to put ourselves or what to do with ourselves. In the dying process there is a transition, and for those around the dying person this can be upsetting as we think there is something wrong. The actual cause is not really known, my sense is when we are in the process of dying our energetic body is feeling confined by our physical body as we are trying to leave. These are only my thoughts regarding this phase. There are medications that can be given to assist someone to relax into the process and this can ease the situation for all concerned.

The following phase is when the dying person moves into a very peaceful state, marked by regular breathing deep in the belly which gradually rises in the chest and then into the back of the neck and throat. At this stage the only movement from the breath can be seen around the throat/mouth. A bit like a fish out of water and then when the breath stops you can hardly tell; it happens peacefully and easily. You are sometimes aware of a rattling sound at the back of the throat and this is called the death rattle and is caused by secretions at the back of the throat, which the dying person has no energy to clear.

We may feel uncomfortable with this and project our discomfort on to the dying person – getting their airways cleared. Here it is important to remember the dying person's experience of their body as they prepare to leave will be different from ours. If the person is breathing comfortably despite the rattle from the secretions then let them continue.

Another part to be aware of is that there is a difference between non-responsive and a coma. A dying person in most cases does not go into a coma. In a coma we are unable to switch between non-responsive and responsive.

A dying person only appears like this because they do not have the energy to respond, but they are aware, able to hear and process what they hear to the very last moments. We hear of cases where the person may choose to respond to special moments like when they have been waiting for someone to come so they can say what they wanted to say before they go. Hearing is the last sense to diminish and this is to be remembered. The dying person whilst appearing non-responsive can hear everything that is said around them.

The moment of death remains a mystery to those of us left behind. Certainly the emotional pull of loved ones may make it difficult to depart this world, this lifetime and yet having loved ones with us may help support us take our crossing. For my mum the crossing was something she had been aware of since she was a young girl. I remember, when I completed my training, I spoke to her about the great death spiral that assists a soul to leave cleanly and consciously from this lifetime. She recounted a time when she witnessed her aunt assist her nan through the crossing and that her nan was saying to her aunt, "I'm crossing, I'm almost there, almost, I'm here," and then she was gone.

Mum understood this part of my shamanic training and I knew she had a sense of the process from her experience that would help her. She also gave me permission to assist her by creating the great death spiral ceremony.

The final week of her life, Mum had been sleeping most of the time. I was back in France and before I had left, Mum and I had spoken. I told her that I would be back the following weekend and that there was no need to wait for me. We said our physical goodbye. The following Friday, the day before I was due back in the UK, Mum, fully conscious, sat upright in bed and declared that she was bored. She asked my brother to go home so that my dad could sleep in the spare room and she requested a Marie Curie nurse to sit with her that evening. At one a.m. the nurse called my dad because my mum had asked for him. My Dad was able to hold my mum's hand as she crossed. She was talking but dad was unable to make out her words and she was gone.

In France I woke up at two a.m. knowing Mum had gone, sensing and touching something I cannot describe. My brother at one a.m. in the UK had a vision of our granddad (my mum's dad) holding the hands of two children and walking away.

The phone rang; it was Dad, I knew. I arrived in the UK eight a.m. Saturday morning. Mum had orchestrated the whole thing and made sure she did it her way with incredible grace. I have so much to thank Mum for and her lessons and wisdom during the dying journey will stay with me always until it is my turn.

I know that we have and will experience the death of loved ones and each experience will be different, depending on circumstances. There is never one answer but the wisdom of the process can help us be of the most service we can be to the person who has, is or will be making that crossing.

There are many books around death and dying. One of the most beautiful books is *Water Bugs and Dragonflies – Explaining Death to Children* by Doris Stickney. It is for children but we all have a child within us. The story itself is a simple and beautiful way to explain something that none of us really remember the answers to. It is the secret that we keep from ourselves.

The shamanic traditions encourage us to know death and to live fully whilst we are here in this physical body. And when it is our time to cross between the worlds we know the way and we can make the crossing consciously. During the training, in the East direction the great death spiral is shared and experienced. It is a map that assists us to know the way home when it is our turn, regardless of the circumstances. Alberto has written about this in his book *Shaman, Healer, Sage*.

The journey continues and the wisdom of these teachings helps us to take those steps necessary to realign our self in our life. To come into a more balanced relationship within. It is important to realize that as we step into the East we step into the place of visionary. We begin to envision our lives into being. Imagine if you have not done the inner work of the South and the West what would you envision? Yep, you guessed it, more of the same but this time in a more powerful way. Why? Because you realize how much power there is in your intention and how much of what you experience you create. What is the point of keeping creating the same when it hurts? Do we want to leave this legacy for our kids to reconcile?

As we come into the East direction, we realize that we want to sit in the centre of our wheel of life, and we begin to recognize that the wheel itself is an incredible map that enables us to look at life from different perspectives. If we look at the wheel and the cardinal points we can see that:

In the South direction we look at the story we identify ourselves by but this of course can be useful in any moment when looking at perhaps one situation in our lives. So this can be a behaviour, a belief, a situation or an emotion. Anything that we find that we are identifying ourselves with to the point that we think this is who we are.

In the West we begin to release and move away from these old patterns, beliefs and behaviours so we begin differentiation. It may be that you begin to realize you are not just a Mum, or like the story I told earlier in the book about my recognition of my projection of selfishness on to my husband. I began to differentiate from the old behaviour once I had recognized the selfishness that lived within me.

In the North we begin to take the wisdom from the situation and integrate this into our life. You may look at old family patterns, for example, and ask yourself, how do I hold them now? What nugget of gold have I integrated into my life? Like the infant who identifies with their family, the adolescent who differentiates from their family and the young adult who integrates back into the family at a new level. Or again as I differentiated from my projection and old behaviours around selfishness I began to integrate what I had learned about myself.

In the East we take that step into our new map, we create that new coordinate that supports our transcendence of our old ways of being. What have you moved beyond? Maybe it is the old story, the role of victim, the role of mother, as you once knew it. You may have one subject, role, belief that belong in two or all the sectors, just like my selfishness. Here in the East I moved beyond all my beliefs, thoughts, feelings and actions associated with selfishness. I no longer experienced my husband or myself as selfish.

Earlier in the book we looked at creating a nature painting and this is something that you can use, knowing that being a circle and held by the cardinal points you can begin to move issues in your nature painting through each different direction on a mythic level whilst at the same time becoming conscious of the beliefs and behaviours. It is so important that we participate for here is the power within each one of us to make the difference.

It would have been all too easy for me to continue to blame my husband for the bad atmosphere and the arguments but by taking a look at myself through the cardinal points of the medicine wheel, I was able to see myself truly and make a change. It wasn't necessary to make a huge elaborate drama around the shift, only a quiet moment of introspection without my rose-tinted glasses.

You can use the medicine wheel with one issue. Perhaps it is a business proposition. All your thoughts and feelings about this proposal can be taken through the four directions. Just by taking the question, emotion, belief, behaviour through the four directions gives you a different perspective. Effectively you will see what you identify with, differentiate from, integrate and transcend. And by moving clockwise you shift energetically and move beyond how you currently hold the situation. It helps you move beyond any preconceived ideas, expectations or false wishes.

Be bold and bring it into a meeting and get everyone to play. I know that business doesn't normally mix with play but maybe with the eyes of a child we can see something that otherwise may have remained hidden and may turn out to be the key to turn things around. Who knows, and you certainly will not if you don't have the experience.

Let's take a business meeting. Whether you are conscious of it or not you are surveying the terrain, the landscape of the meeting and working out where you fit in as a coordinate. This comes from your own preconceived ideas about how this meeting is going to be and to do this you are pulling on past experiences; one to determine where you fit and then to determine what strategy you are going to use. So into your computer archives you go and choose a file that looks similar and you reinstate this coordinate, this strategy because it worked the last time. Depends on what you were basing your decisions on. The trouble is you don't always know exactly where or from whom this strategy originated. By taking ideas or coordinates from the past you limit the possible outcome of the meeting as you have already determined how it will play out and so the outcome is limited to your strategies of the past. The tighter your preconceived ideas are the more firmly set in place are your coordinates, the less room you have to move and explore new possibilities and maybe more advantageous outcomes. And this takes courage because everyone present in the meeting will be doing the same, seeing the meeting from their rose-tinted specs. So to take a different view, you are asking everyone to shift their strategies, and the preservation of their identity and their meeting map coordinates. And there are likely to be those present who may not want to because as far as they are concerned doing it this way they get what they think they want. How great would it be to come out of every meeting feeling alive, energized and feeling full up and enthusiastic?

Well it is possible, you can begin by looking at your own beliefs and behaviours, make a conscious decision to open up your map of meetings and have the courage to be true to who you are on the inside.

For example I remember introducing a talking stick (TS) to a meeting. These were used by Native American Indians during their tribe meetings to ensure everyone present was acknowledged and heard. It is a real discipline. You see, often we are so busy formulating our answers or our side of things that despite others speaking we don't always hear or listen to what they are saying. Using a talking stick means only the person with the talking stick can speak. When they have finished saying what they want to say, the talking stick goes back to the centre of the table. Then the next person who is ready to speak picks up the TS and begins to share their thoughts, etc. You have to stay awake and listen and hear the other person without butting in. It is a great way to observe internally what is going on, you have a moment to notice feelings and if they don't pass through emotions and all that you attach to them. The TS gives a moment to consider your response rather than diving in immediately as if your life depended on it. You get time to notice your internal dialogue, the distraction of the voice of your identity preparing how you will give your contribution.

It gives everyone present the opportunity to observe how energy naturally moves within a meeting and if we're awake enough to see it we will notice that energy automatically moves to the participants. You may notice that everyone is suddenly focused on one person. Energetically it is known that this person has something to share. If they do, great, if not then the possibility has died and the energy will move on. The TS involves everyone, acknowledges everyone and welcomes participation.

A friend and I used this around the dinner table one evening. It was hilarious, but very thought-provoking as we all realized how we so wanted to put our opinion across. We saw the moments when we interrupt because we were already answering before the other person had finished speaking. Wow, what an eye opener. It was easy to see with this discipline in place how people's emotional level of engagement can really interrupt the true flow of a debate.

One step further is to introduce the nature painting. Here you can use a simple object to represent the issue and then everyone present can blow their ideas, their concerns into natural objects and place them in the circle. You can do this naming the thing or silently. Once everyone has participated, take a moment to pause and observe what has been created, inviting everyone to share their feelings. This gives an opportunity for what is really available to show up. You can invite all participants to move objects around, pause, sense how this feels. You can leave the creation and go back to the talking stick and notice that everyone has shifted enough to meet the subject of the meeting at a new level.

It has to be worth the experience. Yes, it takes courage to do things differently, to introduce a new map, and in doing so you can open up opportunities and possibilities you had no idea existed. This is how this practice assists us personally, in our work place and in our lives, when we are willing to open the door to a new experience. Of course if this seems like too big a leap then start with the nature painting, looking at your own personal relationship with your work, your business, your position. Experience this art on a personal level and then take it that next step if you choose. Remember, beliefs can become limiting. Check in every now and then and make room for something new.

As a rule the Q'ero do not drink, but occasionally they will enjoy a beer. We create rules around our beliefs. We want to be able to change the rules occasionally to be open to another possibility, see the expectations and preconceived ideas that we live by, and for a moment try something new and different.

Remember everything is projection; you want to see your projection, own it and tweak it if you want. Remember that significant others will go out of their way to support your projection. Own it, shift it and others will shift too or you will notice a moment of discomfort as everyone learns a new way to behave. Or they will go out of their way to ensure that everything stays as it was and that you stay as you once were. It takes courage and can be uncomfortable but it is easier if you are awake and aware of what is going on.

Summary

As we go around the four directions of the medicine wheel we become more centred within ourselves, within our own wheel, so we become what the shaman call self-referencing. We no longer have to have or need coordinates or a map external to ourselves. We realize our true point of reference in our life is within us, a core intelligence, wisdom and knowledge that we come back to, rather than spending our time looking outside of ourselves for answers or directions. And it gets easier every time we wake up and see ourselves more clearly; as we move around the wheel we become more condensed, our vibration and energy becomes lighter and with lighter energy and less stuff in our suitcases we can find our internal reference point more easily. Our internal wisdom is quite essentially the source of our being.

We still have our everyday routines; life still happens. We still continue to evolve through our experiences and what we learn from them. As a result our vibration is higher and lighter and so creates a very different world to the one we know or have known. Life is more fulfilling even in our daily routines, dealing with the kids, our boss, relationships, our career. The potential for opportunity and possibility exists to create and be living extraordinarily, not just some of the time, in every moment.

There is no one answer
There is no one way
There is not one map
You will remember and then you will forget
Life is like that
Begin with compassion and forgiveness for yourself
Begin to dance with your map of life realizing this is not the territory but your own version of the territory.
Discover who you really are and enjoy participating in creating and living the life you want to experience.
Our journey is effort, dedication and the audacity to do things differently.
Our journey is that we wake up and stay awake
Our journey is reconciliation and balance
Our journey is participating in living and envisioning from a place of reconciliation and harmony
Our journey is growing rainbow bodies, a lightness of being, leaving no tracks, no regrets, a clear back yard.
Our journey is leaving this lifetime consciously complete and whole.

  Many blessings to you on your journey.

  I have been unable to establish the author of this poem that I have chosen to complete this journey. Whoever you are – thank you.

Learning

After a while you learn the subtle difference
Between holding a hand and chaining a soul.
And you learn that love doesn't mean security.
And you begin to learn that kisses aren't contracts
And presents aren't promises
And you begin to accept your defeats
With your head up and your eyes open
And with the grace of an adult, not the
Grief of a child.
And you learn to build all your roads on today
Because tomorrow's ground is too uncertain
For your plans
After a while you learn that even sunshine
Burns if you get too much.
So plant your own garden and decorate
Your own soul – instead of waiting for
Someone to bring you flowers.
And you will learn that you really can endure,
That you really are special.
And that you really do have worth.
So live to learn and know yourself
In doing so, you will learn to live.